"Mandy is a wealth of wisdom and heart. She's able to simplify the esoteric into practical information to bring joy, love, and manifestation into one's life."
— **Kimberly Van Der Beek**,
wellness blogger and environmental rights activist

"Mandy's work is a unique bridge between modern psychology and spirituality delivered with accuracy, compassion, and unconditional love. Among other things, Mandy's teachings give us a deep understanding for our less desired sides so we can be more loving towards ourselves and thus others. This understanding is, in my opinion, what mankind needs so desperately today to heal."
— **Dr. Afsoon Pouya**, coach and
Cognitive Behavioral Therapist, founder of True Vibration Academy

"Having known Mandy Morris for years, I have seen how her techniques impact a person's life. In fact, I have personally experienced the life-changing results of her teachings. Above that, Mandy's ability to improve lives comes from her profound love for all. A love that can transform each of us."
— **Michael Barnes, Ph.D.**, microbiologist,
geneticist, and business coach

"Mandy's profound insights lay out the most important principles to mastering manifestation so you can live out your dreams, manifest a life full of abundance, and put your spiritual understanding into practice."
— **Peter Nguyen**, CEO of Ad Exchange Group,
Ernst & Young National Finalist Entrepreneur of the Year

8
SECRETS
TO
POWERFUL
MANIFESTING

ALSO BY MANDY MORRIS

Love "It's How I Manifest":
On Abundance, Happiness, Joy, and Peace of Mind

8
SECRETS
TO
POWERFUL
MANIFESTING

How to Create the
Reality of Your Dreams

MANDY MORRIS

HAY HOUSE, INC.
Carlsbad, California ✦ New York City
London ✦ Sydney ✦ New Delhi

Published in the United States by: Hay House, Inc.: www.hayhouse.com®
Published in Australia by: Hay House Australia Pty. Ltd.: www.hayhouse.com.au
Published in the United Kingdom by: Hay House UK, Ltd.: www.hayhouse.co.uk
Published in India by: Hay House Publishers India: www.hayhouse.co.in

Project editor: Melody Guy
Cover design: Barbara LeVan Fisher
Interior design: Claudine Mansour Design

Cataloging-in-Publication Data is on file at the Library of Congress

Hardcover ISBN: 978-1-4019-6495-5
E-book ISBN: 978-1-4019-6503-7
Audiobook ISBN: 978-1-4019-6504-4

10 9 8 7 6 5 4 3 2
1st edition, March 2022
Printed in the United States of America

SUSTAINABLE FORESTRY INITIATIVE
Certified Chain of Custody
Promoting Sustainable Forestry
www.sfiprogram.org
SFI-01268
SFI label applies to the text stock

For Oliver, Braydon, Zion, and Mom,
who spin my world on its axis.
I am everything because of you.
And for my Authentic Lifers, who've given me
a reason to serve with gratitude and love.

CONTENTS

INTRODUCTION

Don't You Love a Good Secret?

Every single one of us knows the confusion, sadness, and frustration that comes with feeling like life just isn't working out in the way that we think it should. Maybe you feel lost or burdened by events from your past. Perhaps your relationships haven't turned out how you'd expected. Let me guess: you aren't exactly crushing it at work, and your finances are less than ideal. Listen, I get it. I really do. Because if you're anything like I once was, there's a good chance that you've prayed for a different reality than the one you're currently living, or you tried to manifest a brighter future all on your own, only to end up where you began—feeling defeated, inadequate, insecure, hopeless, and unloved. I always thought there was something wrong with me when I battled these demons since it seemed like others were able to have or do the things that I wanted for myself.

Well, I'm here to tell you that life doesn't have to be this way— that you can have everything you've ever desired, and then some. I know because I'm now on the other side of this pain. After overcoming challenges in just about every area of my life, I've taught millions of others that everything they want is available to them, and there's always a path to get there.

Yes, *always*.

As an entrepreneur, philanthropist, and manifestation expert, I've spent close to a decade teaching clients—privately, online, and during life-changing live events and workshops with my company Authentic Living—how to have a genuine and deeply fulfilling existence so that they can manifest instant and lasting change. Time and again I've seen that abundance, happiness, love, and purpose will find its way to you when you are in an honest, healthy mindset that puts you on your highest and clearest energetic path—one that reveals itself when you understand, purify, and elevate the beliefs that guide you. Once you begin to embrace who you authentically are, you become whole and complete from following your soul's true north. Your manifestations become more beautiful and easily achieved than you could ever imagine.

What are the specific keys to your sought-after future? Eight secret principles that will help you reach your greatest desires with ease and speed. They'll point the way to your most spectacular self, which is aligned with the universe's highest good, and the result will become the foundation for manifesting any and every goal that you wish to accomplish. The methods that I share in this book were primarily pulled from and developed while I was in an intuitive and meditative state. I've been gathering information this way since the age of five, and I believe that what I access and teach comes from a pure, divine source. While I am not a psychic or medium, I—like most thought leaders who are tapped into their spiritual side—am constantly given guidance and direction from the universe, and much of that wise intelligence has included how to teach manifesting to the masses in a fresh, unique way. I take this mission very seriously. My techniques are also inspired by my formal education; research I've done alongside notable scientists, doctors, and psychiatric nurses; and personal experiences that have changed my own trajectory. I've learned a lot from partnering with clients who have come to me at their lowest moments too. After they've worked with me to enhance their thoughts, rewire their brains, and finesse their intentions, they've gone on to manifest the home, romantic partnership, career, health, vacation, financial stability, purpose work, family, and (enter heartfelt craving here!) of their wildest dreams.

Unlocking the Secrets to Manifesting

Though I've never been happier and felt more carefree thanks to my manifesting secrets, life wasn't always smooth sailing. My journey has been riddled with family dysfunction, addiction, divorce, sexual trauma, eating disorders, and too many dead-end relationships and jobs to count. As you'll soon read in more detail, after an abusive boyfriend brought me to my knees, I knew that something about my path had to change—and I did everything in my power to forge a new path. I surrendered to a higher power, earned professional degrees in psychology and leadership to bolster my spiritual growth, and felt guided to channel and implement select ways that science and neurology affect our ability to manifest. (To be honest, I initially didn't realize how scientifically aligned a lot of this information was until highly intelligent friends validated that I must be pulling from a divine place since I had no formal background in the specific and seemingly innate wisdom I was sharing.)

When I began to pursue a Ph.D., I realized that more education wasn't actually the best route for me, so I opted out. Honestly, all the schooling in the world couldn't heal or help me move forward in my life; instead, I instinctively knew that I had to figure it out on my own. So much of what I do is driven by an internal compass that if something doesn't feel right, I just don't do it. Based on divine guidance that I received during meditation, however, I came to learn that fixing myself with a higher power's help made manifesting easier, and as I examined how and why my life was getting better, the eight secrets emerged. I felt so good operating by these guideposts that I couldn't keep this information to myself and began sharing it with as many people as I could. And now, I can't wait to share these secrets with you!

Doing the Inner Work

Forget colorful vision boards and generic positive thinking. More than anything else, I've found that manifestation requires staying in alignment with your healthiest and most authentic self—and that takes some prep. Before you can even set an intention to put the right manifesting wheels into smooth motion, you have to spend some time recognizing and then removing the defeating beliefs, thoughts, and feelings that generate low-frequency energy. These can block your goals and make upsetting outcomes occur. It's a phenomenon that I call "counter-manifesting," in which you accidentally create a life that you *don't* want because you're living in emotional and energetic disarray. However, when you're able to revise and boost your beliefs, thoughts, and feelings, which can get you into a higher vibrational state, the universe will respond in kind. Whatever you want will start showing up in a positive way since you're doing the work that allows you to heal sabotaging beliefs, create new ones, and move on from past traumas that get in the way of your goals. Once you're in that genuinely positive state, *then* you're speaking the universe's language! At the same time, your new and improved beliefs carve out fresh neuropathways in the brain so that your upgraded thoughts and behaviors become your new normal and automatic, emotional go-to. You move the manifesting needle on every level: mental, emotional, physical, spiritual. In no time at all, your new way of living becomes a habit, and manifesting is a breeze. Consciousness, after all, is one of the strongest forces in the universe, and while every one of us has a human story that's peppered by our past, we can decide to either succumb to it or transmute it for a better future. If your consciousness is directed toward the past, then it is refeeding that past, and that monster will become even more energetically dense. But if you choose to change and reframe that human story, then your consciousness will no longer be present in those past moments, and no longer exist. Just like that. It's so profound when this happens that I can't think of any words to explain how it feels. What I do know is that you will experience a deep taste of the truth—which feels light and freeing and loving and complete—so much so that it's actually painful to live any other way. You will realize that your life can reflect who you choose to be, and that version is not who you've been in the past, but who you authentically are.

How to Use This Book

I want you to get the most out of this book that you can as I explain the basic tenets of manifesting and then dive into the eight secrets that will turn your life around. Though some of these steps include tools that you can use at any point in the process, they are rather sequential, so you should read and practice them in order. For maximum results, you'll also want to be sure that you fully understand and have implemented each principle before moving to the next. Eventually, you can customize the manifesting process to suit your goals based on what's worked best for you in the past. But while you're still learning, I ask that you practice this in an orderly way.

Here's a sense of how your process and growth will play out as we work together. I want to lay this out now, so you can envision how all the small, moving parts will work toward a beautiful and synergistic whole. In Part I of this book, I'll share my personal story, plus the principles and science behind manifestation in general, and then in Part II, I'll explain the eight manifesting secrets and suggest ways for you to apply and customize them for your own life. Throughout the book, I'll teach you how to check in with your existing beliefs, thoughts, and feelings—as you experience them—so that you can revamp them, build new neuropathways in your brain to support them, and raise the energy that feeds them until the process becomes second nature.

Don't worry—I will make it fun and fascinating so that you enjoy the process as you go! I'll help you detangle the dense energy and negative blocks that get in the way of your goals. I'll also help you manage upsetting reminders from your past with "pattern interrupts," which shift your emotions and redirect your energy when you react negatively to a trigger. You'll improve your ability to practice self-love and create the kind of intentional energy you need to manifest. At this point, you will begin to name and set your manifesting goals, plus create a "manifestation blueprint" to help you take the guided steps that turn your hopes into a remarkable reality. With your manifestations now in motion, you'll then rewrite the remaining rules, or beliefs, that you live by and learn to tap into a future version of yourself that can help you solve problems going forward. These last two steps position you to receive miraculous events without much of a concerted effort, thanks to the consistent, elevated vibration that you now embody. Wonderful events and conversations will fall in your lap from this point on, since you will exist and zoom along on a vibration where only the best stuff is available. Your partnership with the universe will be stronger than it's ever been. You will know how to co-create with divine energy, and you will do it with ease and frequency.

One last note that I'd like you to keep in mind as you read: I reference God a lot in this book as I believe that God is in ultimate command of all that we manifest and co-create. I do not attach male or female pronouns to God because I believe that God is the source of all divine, creative energy and does not have a gender. So that being said, know that *God* is simply the term I use to refer to my higher power. You may instead prefer to call God by other names like Source, Universe (I use this a lot too), what have you. God's wisdom and love will remain awesome and limitless, no matter what name you choose to use when talking about this energy.

By picking up this book, you have made a powerful choice to change your life for the better—for you, and everyone around you too. While I'll admit that it's a pretty comprehensive read, I've also packed it with tons of love and encouragement because I'm so honored that we get to change your life together. The concepts, tools, and eight secrets themselves will move you into a greater reality and place you firmly in charge of all your circumstances as they unfold and improve, each and every day. So let's not waste another second: it's time to rock and roll.

Part I

BENDING TIME

Chapter 1

FROM MAYHEM
TO MAGIC

Sometimes our deepest pain and trauma can help us discover who we were born to be. The situations that got us there may not be pretty, but the potential to transform them into something worthwhile and fulfilling can lead to a beautiful existence—one that enhances who we are and helps others too. For so much of my life, I was a slave to the inner turmoil that came from living through painful and highly emotional experiences, and as a result, I unconsciously created a life that was riddled with even more struggle, heartache, fear, and shame. I was finally able to turn my ship around when I discovered, and then thoughtfully implemented, the secrets I'm revealing in this book. They led me to a place of deep self-awareness, which helped me manifest my heart's desires and watch miracles effortlessly unfold.

The life of *your* dreams is also within reach, and I can't wait to help you get there. But first, I'd love to share my story so that you can get a sense of what I had to overcome. I've left out some of the more private details to protect loved ones, but I hope that what I do reveal is enough to help you feel, deep down in your bones, that if I could come out on top, you can too.

The Call That Changed Everything

I still remember my own transformation clearly. It began the day I shut off my inner light.

When I was 13 years old, a close friend of mine died from a sudden brain aneurism, and on the same afternoon as his funeral, I received a call from my father, whose voice sounded defeated, strained, and downright sad—clearly, something was very wrong. I asked him why he sounded so overwhelmed with sorrow and exhaustion, and he simply said, "Honey, Daddy is just tired. Tell your sister I love her so much." Even at 13, I could intuitively feel the weight of my father's few words and inferred that he was going to harm himself.

He was calling to say good-bye.

I froze and immediately internalized the experience. I didn't cry or scream for him to call 911; instead, it felt as if my heart dropped into my stomach, and I became overcome with guilt, confusion, and regret. I thought that if I had just been with my father before he made the decision to take his life and tell him that his soul was marvelous and all his mistakes were forgiven—if I could have just convinced him that he was worthy of abundant, unconditional love—then that phone call, and the bottle of pills he swallowed leading up to it, would have never happened.

Growing up, I didn't know that my father wrestled with his share of demons. He never dealt with childhood trauma, felt shame around his romantic relationships, and hid deep feelings of inadequacy. Like most little girls, I thought that my father was big and strong and could handle anything that life threw at him. I thought

Daddy was brave and invincible. He was my world and one of my greatest sources of love—yet little did I know that love was exactly what my father craved most from others and himself. He needed to feel absolved of his past, but I didn't understand that this was nobody's job but his own. That beyond suicide, there was another way.

I feel grateful and downright lucky that my father didn't die that day. Thanks to my mom, who grabbed the phone from me and called an ambulance and then screamed for him to tell her where he was and to not involve me and my sister in this harrowing moment, my dad survived his overdose. After the paramedics pumped Dad's stomach, and he had a cigarette, he called to say that he'd be okay.

This experience turned my life upside down. It made me feel so helpless and cut right to my soul. As a child of divorce, I already blamed myself for a lot of emotional situations that actually had nothing to do with me. So that day I managed to somehow feel responsible for Dad's sorrow and emptiness, berate myself for not being there to stop his suicide attempt, and then take it all a step further to wonder why I wasn't lovable enough for Dad to want to stay on earth with me. It's this last point that morphed into a self-flagellating loop that stuck with me as time went on: *Why would Dad leave me behind? Am I not good enough? What's wrong with me?*

Dad's suicide attempt made me feel disposable as a daughter, and as a person, which made living feel inevitably pointless as an endeavor. I remember thinking that if things could get so bad for my father, who was such a pillar of strength to me, and force him to collapse and crumble to the point of wanting to die, then I wanted no part of it. If someone as wonderful as Dad couldn't push through the loneliness or emotional burdens or whatever it was that broke him down, then I didn't want to face what life had in store for someone clearly as unlovable as me.

And just like that, I chose to mentally opt out. I began to abandon the essence of who I'd been up to that point and who I was in my soul. I became a shadow of my former promising self.

Before the World Went Dim

Prior to losing my way, I was full of positive energy and shining potential. Whether it came from a teacher, neighbor, or stranger on the street, Mom said she was always being told "there's something special about Mandy." For instance, my mom loves to tell how, when I was three, I opened up the Bible one day and began to perfectly read the words in front of me! Around the same time, my preschool teacher told Mom that she felt I was extremely advanced, and because the preschool had an existing partnership with a local university for gifted children, she suggested I join. There, they'd test my IQ and create a program to enhance my aptitude. But Mom was afraid to push me too hard and instead encouraged me to be a "normal kid." My father and his side of the family were all very intelligent but also claimed to suffer from their overanalytical minds. Mom did not want the same foreboding future for me.

My great-grandfather and father had brilliant brains that were vulnerable to addiction. My great-grandfather was a brick layer; after spying a tall building, he was said to immediately be able to tell you how many bricks were used to make it. And according to family lore, he was also an inventor, with patents on all kinds of bricklaying equipment. Too bad he sold his patents for a few bucks or a couple bottles of booze, since he'd drink to numb out his all-consuming and hyperactive thoughts. My dad was also very bright and had an impressive photographic memory. When he worked as an oil landman, whose job was to negotiate with landowners so that his company could operate or drill on their property, Mom said he could read pages of highly specific maps and land descriptions and recall every detail without a second glance. Dad was also a wiz at trivia games and riddles. But neither man had positive role models or felt the love they needed to flourish, so they self-destructed using pills or alcohol to shut down their minds.

Given these men's legacies, Mom taught me instead to value my heart over my brain and made me feel that being a good person and doing the right thing was as, if not more, important than academics. In this way, she gave me the space to tap into my true nature—divine and unconditional love. Even my elementary school teachers noticed how naturally love flowed from me and used it to help others. Kids with special needs or anger issues, for instance, would calm down by just being in my presence. Teachers would often pair me with troublemakers to ease their worries. I began to see myself as a girl who could help others; people felt better around me, and my love proved to be enough to calm anyone down. Just by being myself, *I* was enough.

So imagine my shock and despair when my father's suicide attempt implied otherwise. It's no wonder I spiraled into feelings of self-judgment, confusion, guilt, inadequacy, and anger.

Weeks after my dad's suicide attempt, I began earning bad grades, dropped out of gifted programs at school, and stopped caring so much about others. I used to love playing piano and guitar, but I turned away from these interests. I refused to do school sports, even though I was naturally athletic and loved volleyball, soccer, football, cheerleading, dance, and gymnastics.

I'll never forget when one of my high school history teachers pulled me aside to say, "What has happened to you? You'll go nowhere if you don't start caring about your future." When I heard my teacher's comment, I remember smiling inside and defiantly thinking *Yes, I want to go nowhere. You can't make me care, and I'm done trying. What's the point?*

If I'd dug a little deeper at the time, I'd have realized that what I was *really* feeling was *If I couldn't save my own dad, then what's the point?* I wanted to become invisible so that nobody would ask for my help—the help that my father didn't seem to value enough to ask for. And if I closed my heart off, I wouldn't have to feel any more pain for any reason. But as it turns out, when you block out all of your painful emotions, you block out love and all of the positive ones too. And when you try to hide and become invisible, you just draw people into your world who are like-minded in the worst way. The lights go out, and you're surrounded by darkness. Eventually you forget that you *are* light, and you start thinking that darkness is all there is. You lose who you are, until one day you don't recognize who you see in the mirror anymore.

I Could Run, but I Couldn't Hide

Throughout high school, the last thing I wanted was to be with my thoughts and feelings. It was too painful, so instead I chased distraction and variety. And the faster I ran away, the better. This led to a lot of change and instability, which became such a constant for me—with friends, grades, my identity, relationships, cars, eating disorders, you name it—that I became a master at looking for unstable situations that offered novelty and instant gratification. I loved chasing a high and never getting too comfortable. I liked feeling good in the moment and then moving on, by choice, without giving life the chance to take something away from me first.

After graduation, however, I left home—and my parents made it clear that the minute I walked out their door, I was completely on my own. Given that I had no choice but to sink or swim, I decided that I'd try to make something of my life. I hustled, working three jobs so that I could pay tuition at a state university. At one, I worked in a scrapyard, moving tires, pulling parts, and checking in scrap vehicles. It was grueling work. I also began excelling at school for the first time since my dad's overdose, but this didn't mean life got any easier. I still had to sleep in my car a few nights, needed others to buy me food and gas, and felt ashamed of my situation. I was making an earnest effort to get ahead, but no matter what I did, I couldn't seem to feel settled, happy, or fulfilled.

Too low on funds to continue paying state tuition, I transferred to a community college and eventually Grand Canyon University, where I managed to pay my tuition in full by working as an education counselor for the college. Here, things began looking up. I earned my bachelor's degree in psychology and master's in business leadership. For the first time in a while, I found myself at the top of my game—making what I felt was good money, doing well at work, eating clean, and exercising a lot. I also worked hard to put my bulimia, which I'd developed in high school after yet another dysfunctional relationship, in the rearview mirror for good too.

Though I was now trying to be the best version of myself that I could, I didn't realize that to have a good life, my mental health mattered. I thought that collecting credentials and accomplishments would get me far enough since that's what society valued. And on the outside, I looked all right. But on the inside, I felt like a wreck because I didn't have the tools to break free from my past. I continued to make poor emotional choices for myself because a toxic cycle was my normal. Opening my heart to good people or feeling deep, genuine connections felt unsafe. I ended up in situations and relationships that were dangerous and destructive to my soul, and I blamed and shamed myself for it—which further created a lack of self-love. I hid this from the outside world. If nobody noticed I was falling apart, this was safer than being honest about it.

I hit rock bottom when, in my 20s, I dated one of the most maladjusted and abusive men I've ever known. This boyfriend would get drunk, call me disgusting names, and show me photos of the women he'd slept with when we were fighting. He'd then apologize and "show remorse," so I'd cave and forgive him. I became used to this abusive cycle, tried to fix him, and even attempted to mirror his behavior. I was so used to confusing pleasure with pain that I accepted his treatment for too long. We broke up and got back together for two years.

In search of a fresh start, I finally moved to Florida, but this same boyfriend soon joined me there. After an especially tough day, he threw a glass of red wine at me during a fight. The glass shattered on the wall behind me and the wine bled into the carpet. In that moment, the realization of my deep lack of self-worth came over me as a heavy veil of denial also began to simultaneously lift. I thought *How could I let this happen to me? How did I get here? How poorly do I think of myself to take this for so long?* I could see his rage and the unresolved hurt in his face. I didn't love this man the way he wanted me to, and it was killing him. I finally understood and screamed, "Get out! Get out of my life!" He left. This was the last time I'd lay myself at the altar of turmoil.

Enough was enough.

Nowhere to Go but Up

For the first time, I realized that running away from my problems didn't work. It made everything worse. By not dealing and healing from the trauma with my dad, and my past, it just re-created itself in the present. Just as my dad attempted to run from his own shame and inadequacies by chasing women, drugs, alcohol, and ultimately suicide—to distract himself from his own thoughts and feelings—I was doing the same but with different diversions. A lot of the men I dated, in fact, were like my father. What Dad craved and needed most was to love himself. And I needed the same. I owed myself love that I denied my soul for too long—the innocent, childlike love that was my most authentic and natural state. I needed to find my way back to *me* again.

After my abusive boyfriend left my apartment for good, I fell to my knees and cried. My body heaved as I released the weight of countless, unhealthy decisions. I examined which paths were not my fault and which choices were. Once and for all, I vowed to get my act together.

I dragged my body to the bathroom, staring at my reflection in the mirror, in search of someone that I recognized. I was shocked to find her. I looked into my own crystal blue eyes and saw myself as the pure, limitless potential that God had created my soul to be. I surrendered to the universe and devoted myself to the betterment of the world. I made a vow to God: "I promise humanity that I will show up. I'm here for a reason, so please show me the way, and I will follow it. I don't need anything—not money, a relationship, or children—but please, give me peace."

In that moment, I gave myself over to being a vessel of love for others and said that I would give everything I had to helping people and doing what I was sent here to do. Though I didn't fully grasp the capacity or context, in my heart, I knew that I wanted to use my trauma to help others who'd been where I'd been. I knew that if I could build new beliefs and perceptions, I could meet other people in their pain and help them out. I've never been a very religious person, but I always believed in having my own connection to God. I upheld certain spiritual principles like love, faith, honesty, and integrity in my own way. Now here I was, making my bathroom-mirror commitment to the universe's direction and feeling more secure than ever. I felt an extraordinary sense of love, serenity, and guidance envelop me like I never have before. I faithfully trusted in a higher power to help me take my next steps; clearly, leaning on my own confusing guidance, based on past conditioning, had been ruining me.

New Beginnings

What happened next was nothing short of a miracle. In the following days, my energy shifted so much that I felt as if I were being steered by an inspiring, mighty power both in and around me. I don't know if a higher power showed up so strongly because I'd dedicated my life to service, my intention to change was so earnest, or it was just a random miracle—but I was *all in*. I prayed to whomever was listening, "Remove all that is not meant for me, and bring me all I need to do my work." I didn't know it at the time, but I was adjusting my intentional energy through this mindset. I was vowing to let go of the past and sense of control, so I could purely serve and achieve what I was meant to do.

In no time, I met inspiring people who were healthy and loving, who upheld the best motives and appreciated my light without wanting to control or snuff it out. I read about quantum mechanics and metaphysics and could feel my natural intellect reemerging. I developed loose but effective manifesting techniques, guided by insights that I intuited while meditating. I remembered my poor choices and that I'd hurt others as a by-product of unprocessed pain and mental anguish; my compassion for those in my position grew immensely. I remet my soul and the pure loving being I was. I spent time channeling, as best I could, to be sure I was divinely guided.

Now, channeling wasn't new for me, but I hadn't yet polished this gift. As a kid, I saw spirits and energy and heard noises that no one else could. Around 20 years old, I dropped into a channel in front of a spiritually minded friend—my mouth just opened and words poured out—so he bought me a book on the topic, but it still scared me. I was afraid something dark would get hold of me! However, if I didn't let the information flow, my forehead ached. So I learned to use love to ensure that I only channeled divine information that came from God.

As a new life unfurled before me, it became an amazing, wild ride. I learned to live in the present, which calmed my mind; and if I didn't look too far back or ahead, I could breathe. The universe also dropped little bread crumbs of guidance that led me toward promising opportunities and encounters. While still in Florida, I created videos for my personal social media pages to connect with others. In these videos, I'd share what I learned about the frequency of emotions, the energy behind words, and then use my psychology background to tie it together. I'd share what I learned during channeling and meditation as well. Making these videos let me express myself and expand my community. It was during meditation, in fact, when the eight secrets began to gradually emerge, though I didn't fully put it together as to how they impacted manifestation. I was mainly on a self-healing journey, but it was becoming clear that the more I dealt with the past, the easier it became to create a life that I finally wanted to live. I began to deeply love myself and accept that I was enough—and boy, did life get epic, fast.

Ask and You Shall Receive

I like to think that my bathroom-mirror plea for help was received by God like "Okay, Mandy. I will use you as a vessel. You do your part, and I'll do mine." Because not long after I opened myself up to a more spiritual and service-based existence, my husband, Oliver, showed up. Everything became much more beautiful when he was around. He accepted all parts of me, was so kind, and became my best friend immediately. He'd say, "I love the rainbow of Mandy." It was alongside Oliver, my soul mate, that I was able to burst into the person I am today.

I felt an instinctual pull toward Oliver, as if I knew him on a deeper, soul level. He felt familiar in a way that felt safe and warm. Oliver, who is also a naturally gifted energy healer, was quietly practicing his abilities on family and friends at the time. One night, he did a healing on me. I remember feeling a cosmic connection to this wonderful new friend. We talked about the universe and our purpose work on this planet. He filled a spiritual void, and I relished it.

A few days later, Oliver told me that he'd bought me a gift that was waiting for me at a small store in town. It was a book about the type of channeling that he felt I'd been doing all this time, with a beautiful sunset on the cover. As I was driving home after picking it up, I was amazed to look out my car window and see that the sunset in the sky exactly matched the one on the book's cover. I knew that the universe was intervening in our lives in a special way.

An Authentic Pursuit

Together, Oliver and I moved to Sedona. This town is known as a spiritual hub, so it's no surprise that with dedication on my part, my spiritual gifts amplified there at lightning-fast speed. Almost every day, I would channel information that I felt the world needed to hear and then feel compelled to create a video or reach out to a friend in need—whatever felt aligned with my soul.

I'd begin each day (and still do!) with a simple question for the universe: *What does the world need from me today that I can readily and easily give?* When I'd receive an answer, I'd act on it and feel ready to welcome any good that I had coming my way, without guilt or hesitation.

I continued healing my family relationships and other traumas by using tools that I'd been gathering through meditation and my psychology degree—primarily focusing on manifestation techniques, compassion, clarity, understanding relationship dynamics, and a willingness to focus on the now. I observed what I was telling myself, recognized my beliefs, and realized that if I could break from the ruinous ones, I could revise them and ultimately be free. It wasn't easy. Often, I'd need to have difficult conversations, put up boundaries, remove people from my world, and dig into my own issues, shame, and guilt. But I had a promise to fulfill to God, so playing small or falling back into outdated beliefs and thoughts was no longer an option.

I felt an outpouring of radical empathy, compassion, and forgiveness at the same time, because I now realized that we may be formed by our experiences, but we do not have to be defined by them. My past, for all its pain and heartache, ultimately led me to recognize the core tenets of my current programs: that our past beliefs, thoughts, and feelings impact our personal, energetic vibration, which is related to the quality of life that we manifest for ourselves. So, I examined my feelings, worked on the energy that supported it, and created techniques that helped me manage my triggers with energy that serves the highest good of all. I practiced self-love and fine-tuned what it meant to have the right intentional energy behind a goal and take proactive, divinely led steps toward what you want. Doing all this work is what allowed me to bring my goals to life and create an ideal emotional foundation for manifesting.

I transformed my traumas into opportunities for growth. My mom and I once had a rocky relationship because she was so busy trying to cope with her own past trauma that I as a kid rarely experienced her authentic self. I've come to appreciate how much she sacrificed and how hard she worked to keep our family going—more than I ever realized. Now, we have an honest, growth-oriented friendship in which we both feel deeply loved. We're best friends, and I consider her to be the strongest woman I know. And right before my dad died from a stroke in 2020, I was able to help him heal some of his unhealthy patterns around love and money, and those talks helped me better process our past. I also began to see which friendships needed to end and generational patterns needed to be broken; I'm told that the latter helped many of my extended family members heal too. And when things felt especially hard, I'd remind myself that I wasn't just doing this for me. I had promised humanity that I'd embody my soul so others could too.

It was in Sedona that I began channeling programs that Oliver encouraged me to share with the world, and I ran my first workshop. My eight secrets were often woven throughout these events, but never really called out as such. Oliver continued to grow his healing abilities and began to activate other people's spiritual gifts—be it as a medium, psychic, healer, what have you. The deeper we dug into our spiritual growth, the more we began to build and pursue our purpose work. Through this organic and intuitive process, I found an incredible amount of success, quickly. I allowed my gifts to show up however the universe wished. Any programs that came from my channelings or came to me when I was embodying unconditional love were huge successes, and every single endeavor came from a very real place of love and authenticity.

My company, my purpose work, and my "baby"—Authentic Living—was born.

I built my business with the aim of helping others, and I didn't take my role lightly. After years of fully diving into all that I wasn't, I now knew exactly who I was. I began to lean almost entirely on divine guidance when creating new programs. I'd ask God, *What kind of program does the world need?* and then funnel down the details until what I intuited could be turned into tangible, teachable subjects. So if God told me that the world needs more love, I'd chip away at this broad concept until it turned into instructible tools that encouraged growth.

Up, Up, and Away!

From Arizona, we traveled and soaked up all that life had to offer us. Authentic Living grew in tandem with my spiritual growth, so naturally, its success tripled or quadrupled every year because the energy was perfectly attached. Our next stop was Scandinavia, where I researched and assisted in healing psychosomatic illnesses with top world scientists, doctors, and psychiatric nurses. This was such an insightful time in my life. In a clinical setting, I learned about, and helped to remedy, deep-seated traumas that had created seemingly impossible-to-heal health issues—from stubborn allergies to heart issues, to liver problems, to Tourette's syndrome, to complicated neurological conditions. I even helped myself while I had access to such great minds and medical technology for support. I had severe fatigue and food sensitivities at the time, and after using one of our high-tech devices to diagnose my condition, I learned that my liver was malfunctioning from so many years of anger suppression. And even as a vegetable eating, rarely drinking, regularly exercising, and otherwise healthy adult, my liver couldn't withstand the decades-long psychosomatic onslaught of my past. Gone unchecked, I believe that I'd have accumulated other health issues as additional organs began to compensate and become taxed. After practicing many of the techniques you'll learn in this book, some technology-based therapy, plus removing gluten and cow's milk from my diet, I made a full recovery.

Once my project ended, Oliver and I moved to Dallas for two years, and then Laguna Beach, California, where we got married and conceived our son, my little angel baby Zion; he was a magical addition to our family, which already included my bonus son, born from my heart, Braydon, from Oliver's prior marriage. In Laguna, the universe began creating incredible, random connections with friends who'd refer us to their peers, and soon, we were frequenting events and galas. They'd ask Oliver to do a healing and then send us to others through word of mouth.

My business continued to rapidly expand, and I was pumping out divine information at breakneck speed. I grew my online courses, certification programs, and events, and Oliver became more public about his healing abilities. Each time I launched a workshop, it would fill immediately. The bread and butter of our business became our certification program where people become certified as a "Love and Authenticity Practitioner," which is essentially a life coach. We tightened our focus even more on coaching my methodologies, while my husband performed his healings, activated our clients' spiritual gifts, and certified others to be healers too.

In no time, celebrities, psychiatrists, coaches, therapists, teachers, doctors, nurses, and even world leaders sought us out. Oliver and I came to realize that manifesting a great business, abundance, and entrepreneurship was an energetic game for us. When we mixed the eight secrets with a genuine desire to serve others on a daily basis, blessings were limitless. Our greatest promise to one another when we met was that we would grow—and grow we did.

In 2019, I felt like something was missing from our world. I sensed that we were being pulled in a vastly different direction, and I had to honor it. I began to wonder *What's next for us?* I started having visions of chickens pecking around on an expanse of land and our beloved soulful community of Authentic Lifers socializing with each other in the same space. Within a week, Oliver and I understood the calling: to invest in a retreat center. We found our dream center in Dolores, Colorado, complete with a 7,500 square foot main lodge, a guest house, and another building with 11 bedrooms and a meeting area. In total, the facility sleeps about 60 people. We've built additional fountains, designed labyrinths, installed a hot tub, and created Zen gardens. It's so beautiful, and the sacred energy matches that of my hopes and visions.

Today, I am so proud to say that Authentic Living is a thriving company that serves millions. We have stopped clients from committing suicide, helped parents heal so that their children will never have to, created amazing coaches and healers, and so much more. One of our proudest achievements is the philanthropic work we do in Oliver's native country, the Philippines, serving orphans, the elderly, and pediatric cancer wards; providing disaster relief; building kitchens for schools; and more. We also provide scholarship programs and food, childhood necessities, rent money, and other essentials to those who need it. We've created Authentic Living scholarship programs too, offering our services to those who can't afford them.

Now, the greatness of my life knows no bounds. I went from fearing the unknown and feeling paralyzed in scarcity to running wild and living in divine faith. I went from having unhealthy relationships to being surrounded by the richest, most loving, and most supportive people. I went from an unfulfilling existence to one of pure, epic passion. I currently live in an authentic space of opportunity, life purpose, and synchronistic magic. I lean on my spirituality based on the highest good of all. And when people ask me how I am where I am, I say that I choose growth every day, make it as fun as I can, and follow whatever my intuition tells me. I surrender to life's twists and have a deeply trusting relationship with God. I play the energy game, which largely means manifesting all I desire. I can accomplish in two months what takes other people 25 years because I partner with my mind and the universe.

At the heart of this journey for *you*—just as it was for me—is the discovery of your authentic self. Once you find it, you can't go back—and you won't want to. It's like having the cheat code to life.

But getting there isn't a quick fix at first, although it becomes instantaneous the more you dig in. The truth is our trauma, thoughts, and beliefs play a huge role in making us who we are and creating what we manifest. So does the science behind manifesting, which I'll share in this book, as it best pertains to impacting your neurology (what I scientifically present is what my spiritual guidance, and the universe, tells me is most related to how manifestation and the eight secrets are linked). More than anything, I encourage you to do the brave work to change your course, the way I changed mine, because that's when your conscious manifestations kick into high gear. Implementing these practices isn't as easy as winning the lotto, but there's no bigger jackpot than healing what holds you back so that life flows as effortlessly as it can.

If you want to design what you wish to create in this life, plus who you desire to be for the world, I want us to work together to make sure you get there. I was put on this planet to serve humanity to the greatest ability that I can, and right now, serving *you* is what's been placed on my heart to do. In the best ways possible, I promise that your life will never be the same. So take a few deep breaths, know that you are loved and supported, and turn the page to begin life anew.

Tips and Takeaways

+ Don't try to escape your problems. Life isn't so scary when you stop running from it.

+ When you surrender to God and trust in a higher power, your next steps will unfold before you.

+ Practice self-love while taking proactive, divinely led strides toward your manifestation goals.

✦ Your trauma and beliefs play a big role in making you who you are and creating what you want.

✦ Choose growth every day, make it as fun as you can, and follow what your intuition tells you.

✦ At the heart of this journey is the discovery of your authentic self.

✦ Your achievements are limitless when your mind partners with the universe. Dream big!

Chapter 2

MANIFESTING 101

Manifestation is the process of creating your reality, be it conscious or unconscious. At its best, I like to think of it as self-mastery. Beautiful, effortless manifestation takes the guesswork out of why life is happening the way that it is, allows you to control the outcome of many situations, and puts you in charge of yourself and your future. Through manifestation, your greatest hopes become tangibly available, and anything you've ever wanted is within reach. You gain the ability to make immediate goals, long-term dreams, and everything in between come true.

The concept of manifesting a meaningful life is not a new topic, but after years of trial and error, plus unlimited divine guidance, I have honed in on precisely what makes this practice work at its greatest potential—and it all comes down to the eight powerful practices that I'll introduce in Part II. These principles include creating ways to energetically check in with yourself; finding ways to seek self-love; detangling the dense energy and negative relationships in your life; and embracing positive, intentional energy in all that you do. It's also essential to manage your psychological triggers with pattern interrupts, take a look at the "rules" you live by and be brave enough to rewrite them, and finally, learn to envision and embody your future self. I am consistently told that no one teaches manifestation the way that I do, and that my eight secrets are the missing links to why the practice is hit or miss for so many.

Now one of the huge factors that makes my manifestation practices unique is that I encourage you to recognize and create the emotional state that will bring about happiness rather than just the 3D "stuff" that you think will make you happy; this way, you can manifest with exactitude and true satisfaction. This is a vital part of creating the manifesting magic that I see so often in my clients' lives! For instance, you may think that you want a mansion on the hill or for your ex to come crying back to you, but when you drill down on your desires, you may find that what you really want is the emotional state that those things create—and not the things themselves. At the heart of these hopes may be a need to feel accomplished or unconditionally loved, and if so, there are many ways a person can get there beyond a fancy home or reunion with an ex. Once you get to that feeling, you may then realize that what you originally wanted was inauthentic and choose to shift your manifestation goals. In turn, this transforms your energy from a desperate, dense, and inauthentic state to one of radiant authenticity that's aligned with your soul. It's from this point that manifestations quickly come to fruition because your energy is at its best and your intentions, pure. In other words, this puts you in a high vibrational state and working with your highest self, which is the most authentic version of you on earth.

When you access your highest self, you manifest with the highest good for all concerned, which further elevates your intentions and even bends time to help manifestations happen faster than they would on their own. I realize that this all might sound like a lot to swallow at once, but don't worry! Throughout this book, I will hold your hand through the necessary phases of this process.

Ultimately, manifesting is not just about getting what you want but also surrendering to the universe's grand MO so that it becomes an intuitive exchange and comfortable detachment from your desired outcome. In this way, you'll bring forth what you want more quickly while in a state of peace and harmony. Such a mindset allows you to be in the flow of existence, and in this high vibrational place, it's nearly impossible to manifest things you don't want or lose your manifestations due to a subconscious that's tainted with negative past programming (more on that later).

For instance, I believe that I manifested my family's first move to Laguna Beach. Because my energy was calm and in alignment with the universe's, all I had to do was write about my desire in my journal, attach a timeline to when I wanted it to happen, and surrender to the process. Voilà! At the exact time I'd requested (and with no idea about how it would happen), we were in our new home! This was a "set it and forget it" manifestation, and it came to pass with little effort because I knew how to partner with the universe to sustain my energy at a level where good things naturally flowed to me. As you master the eight secrets yourself, they'll become a way of life for you too. They'll keep you in a high vibrational space that helps you grow and stay connected to God—which is what's most important.

My life is a walking manifestation. I manifested the birth of my son Zion, having my "bonus son" Braydon come live with us, buying our Colorado retreat center, working with world leaders, making large sums of money when the company needed it, growing our business, buying houses that we've lived in, and even earning this very book deal with the exact publisher I'd aimed for! When I personally manifest and teach the topic, I don't bother with too many affirmations or intense visualizations (there's nothing wrong with these; I just find that they aren't very effective for most of my clients). Instead, journaling works best. If I write down a goal, it happens. I once drew a picture of me in the now, looking sad and confused, and then drew myself six months later with a dollar sign in my hand, lots of hearts surrounding me, and me flying first class in an airplane. Six months to the *day*, Oliver and I flew first class to Dallas—and I hadn't even met him when I wrote that entry!

Want to give this a try? You don't even need a journal for this experiment! Just grab a sheet of paper (even the back of an envelope will do), and draw two pictures: one of you now, and a second that includes a multifaceted goal that you'd like to achieve in six months. For instance, I drew myself at the time, and then a second illustration that represented money, love, travel, and happiness aspirations. Your art skills don't have to be fancy; I like to scribble stick figures using crayons, a pencil, or ballpoint pen. When you're finished, place the drawing in a special drawer or box in your closet, and forget about it. Make a note on your calendar, six months from now, to pull out the illustration and see if any aspects of your manifestation have come true. I suspect that at least one part of your scenario will!

One of the coolest manifestation stories I know, however, was created by Oliver. He used to keep a stock photo of a Rolls-Royce in front of a luxurious home as the screensaver on his computer, as a symbol of the abundance that he hoped to someday achieve. Oliver has always been obsessed with RRs, so years later, when we finally had the means, I bought him one as a very special treat. That same day, we happened to move into our second home in Laguna. Can you believe that when we stood back from the house with the Rolls parked in front, we realized that we'd unknowingly rented *the house* from the stock photo!?

Now, I don't feel that money or luxury are the most important manifestations by any means, but I love this example because it points to how physical matter has been made manifest. I believe that strong finances are just a by-product of sustaining a high frequency, and as long as God means for me to have it and I use it in the highest good of all, I will keep helping others do the same. And while Oliver loves his Rolls, it's worth mentioning that *my* favorite car is the Chevy Suburban I use to haul water and hay from the country farm store back to our retreat center. The moment I channeled that we were meant to transition from our beachy keen life in California to one that insists I spend my days cleaning chicken coops and pulling weeds, I was happy to take that on—and since this was the universe's design, I knew the move would be great.

Manifesting is an important practice that serves so many purposes. It assures you that you're in charge of your world, you're here for a reason, and you can co-create what fulfills you. It proves that you are not a victim of circumstance. If this were the case, based on my past, I'd be a very different person; it's manifestation that's given me a new lease on life. Manifesting also gives your day a pleasant, steady rhythm and sense of predictability, which helps you feel centered. You rarely feel alone because the process increases your awareness that you're part of a larger, universal process; it's an interactive practice that asks you to work with the energy in and around you. Physically, I find that manifesting grants you a clearer mind, more pep, and fewer aches and pains because you're constantly releasing trapped energy that's stuck in your body and field. When manifesting elevates your frequency, whatever is naturally available to you on that wavelength will be amazing. When I gave myself and my future over to God that day, on my knees and in my little apartment, I essentially got myself into the highest vibrational state that I could, and then welcomed whatever came to me next. The end result? A life that's more incredible than I could have imagined or created had I adhered to the world's rules alone.

We're born as infinite beings, so we have unlimited opportunities available to us—that is, if we know how to access them. At Authentic Living, I like to say that so much of our growth comes about because we play the energy game. We don't participate in the human game—a 24/7 grind to kill ourselves or undercut others to get ahead. We manifest our goals, act on opportunities that inspire us, and wait for God to lay out our next steps so that we can rise to the occasion and accomplish what needs to get done. We work with those who are like-minded, with no sense of competition between us. To me, a perfect life is to feel God's presence in everything I do, and that's high vibrational living. The best manifesters I know are those as close to God as possible. The worst are those who consider themselves alone and separate from the universe.

There are three primary components to my personal philosophy of manifestation: the psychological, the scientific, and the spiritual. To be a balanced and highly effective manifester, you need to embrace all three.

Unraveling the Past

Let's first talk about the psychological mechanisms of manifestation, particularly your past programming: the beliefs, thoughts, and traumas that influence your ability to consciously co-create. These factors carry equal weight in how they influence the manifestation process but vary with each person as to which hold you back the most. They also influence counter-manifesting, the process by which you manifest from a troubled unconscious. Counter-manifesting naturally releases the kind of blocked energy that gets in the way of making your most positive dreams come true. When you try to manifest with unhealed and blocked energy, your energy remains heavy and good manifestations rarely occur, but when you deal with the psychological mechanisms of manifestation that hold you back, this raises your vibration and gives you access to the goals that you're longing to receive from the universe's gracious hands.

Your reality is the embodiment of your psyche's programming, and programming from your past has the power to keep positive manifestations from rising to the forefront of your mind. I use the phrase *past programming* a lot as an umbrella term, under which all your beliefs, thoughts, and traumas mix and mingle. Past programming includes societal, religious, cultural, and circumstantial influences that have occurred throughout your life too. They're the values, inklings, preferences, and perspectives with which you were raised and that have shaped your worldview from a young age until now. That said, your mind and its programming work in tandem with your energy field and the universe to bring about manifestations so when negative programming is dominant, your field mostly picks up on this. And just like that, your past runs the show, and you end up counter-manifesting your reality no matter how many candles you light, meditations you do, and spiritual exercises you try. What's more, past programming is often buried deep in your unconscious, so it takes work to understand and replace the imprints it's made.

As you work through the eight secrets and begin to easily grasp my manifestation techniques, you'll start to examine your beliefs and thoughts so that you can learn how to manifest from a high vibrational space. Beliefs comprise your identity and are at the root of who you are. They define what you think is true. And then, thoughts stem from there. For instance, a belief might be that love doesn't last or that the world is unjust, and from there, a thought might be that a stranger is looking at you funny or that you'll never succeed at your job. What's cool is that your thoughts have a frequency, so if you change your thoughts, you can change your energy. And when you emit a higher, more positive frequency to the universe, it responds in kind. So, lighter thoughts create higher thought and energy frequencies that are compatible with the manifestation process, which will make co-creating with the universe a snap. Got it?

Now I need to be clear on a key point about thoughts. As with beliefs, you can't *just* change your thoughts. You have to consider

why you think what you do and work through your past programming until you can frame your thoughts in a new light. This is what
helps you think differently and allows a positive outcome to naturally follow. Having the intention to "be more positive," and then
doing your best at it, is not enough. Positive thoughts must come
from an honest place to raise your vibration to a level that resonates
with the energy it takes to manifest.

You also have to deal with traumas. These are often at the center
of beliefs and thoughts. They're your response to a deeply upsetting
event that overwhelms your ability to cope, lowers your self-esteem,
causes hopelessness, makes you feel loss, causes you to lose control,
can make you feel betrayed or powerless, and can cause incredible
pain and confusion. Fortunately, you don't have to remember or relive the trauma in order to heal it as most therapists would suggest;
but you do have to address the belief that was created because of
the trauma as that is what you have the power and ability to change
in the now.

When a traumatic event imprints itself on your memory, it influences how you see the world and causes you to live in a disempow-
ered state. Unless you've done the work to stop this from happening,
you then unconsciously spend the rest of your life trying to avoid
similar feelings, conversations, or events that trigger the original
memory that's now influenced how you engage with the world. If,
for instance, you were raped, it might create the belief that life is
unsafe, which creates a thought that every man or woman wants to
abuse you. The trauma unconsciously dictates your decisions and
reality, and here's the double whammy: the beliefs and thoughts
that stem from the trauma *aren't always true.* I worked with a client who was repeatedly raped as a child, and every time her husband would lovingly wrap his arms around her from behind, she
would startle or scream. The more he caught her unaware like this,
the more it harmed their marriage because the action brought the

woman back to her original trauma—and this time, with false beliefs and thoughts attached to it. It was such an automatic response that she didn't even realize that she was being triggered from her past. Her husband obviously meant her no harm and had only the best intentions when he tried to embrace her. But you can see how a loud, painful, and deep-seated trauma can grow into an unwieldy mess that makes it impossible to manifest anything at a high vibrational state when you're at the mercy of distressful moments.

Can you think of a time when you overreacted during a conflict with, say, a family member or co-worker that was prompted by a past experience? What were you telling yourself during that squabble, and do you feel the same about it now? Find a quiet spot to think about this scenario, what programming fed the misunderstanding, and imagine how a better outcome might have played out. You can even journal about this or write a letter to this person— that you don't need to send—to simply release that energy from your mental and emotional fields.

We'll get into more specific exercises in Part II of this book, but while we're on the topic of past programming, I'd like to share an excellent one now to whet your appetite and ground you when you've encountered a limiting belief, thought, or trauma. What I'd like you to do is create an umbrella statement about the kind of life you want and write it down in a journal, on a sticky note, or in some other place that you can regularly turn to. For instance, my umbrella statement is "I live a life of love, integrity, growth, and service to others." My client who I just mentioned might write a statement like "I am safe, unbroken, and fully capable of living a beautiful life that's filled with love." Then, as you're making various decisions throughout the day, particularly those that carry weight, ask yourself if the choices you're about to make are in alignment with this statement. If not, what choices can you make to help you get back on track? You might be really frustrated with a family member or feel tempted to quit a project, but before you do anything, consider whether your thoughts and actions align with your umbrella statement and what steps you need to take to keep you anchored in that stable and content place. This tactic immediately helps you to readjust your past programming and its related frequencies, amplifying the most authentic version of you and your soul for all the world to see and experience.

Once you've managed the chaos around and inside you, past programming begins to feel like a past life—it's that far away from your consciousness. And then, if a problem does show up, you will be able to manage additional upheaval in a healthy and productive way, unlike in the past. Instead of scratching the surface every time an obstacle presents itself, you actually peel away the layers of why you behave the way that you do, and eventually the obstacle becomes healed at its root and no longer exists. Throughout this book, you'll learn so much about yourself and how you respond to triggers in everyday life. When you change the way you react to things, the things you react to change, and the energy that helps you manifest your future alters so that it's poised to work to your advantage, for the highest good of all.

So Where Does the Science Come In?

The next key that propels manifesting is the scientific aspect, which mainly includes quantum physics and neuroscience. Now this can get really heady, so when I channeled this information, my divine guidance showed me that I need to keep it simple, limited, and relatable to only the techniques that I teach. I'll dive into more think-y detail in Chapter 3; for now, let's touch on how scientific factors influence the mental and vibrational states that ignite manifestations.

As I've mentioned, all things in this world have a vibration or frequency. And because beliefs, thoughts, traumas, and memories all induce a vibration, any of these can hold you in a certain vibrational state—be it high (positive) or low (negative). Our 3D world is vibrationally dense, and if manifestation is about co-creating here, then it makes sense that when atoms—which are in the solids, liquids, gases, and plasma that make up the "stuff" of our universe—move at a higher rate, this "stuff" manifests faster. On the other hand, disempowering past programming has a low vibration that can create heavy energy that moves more slowly. Not only does this encourage counter-manifesting, but it can create unhealthy blockages in your energy field. These blockages can wreak real havoc. As you know, they slow down your efforts to manifest positive, desired outcomes. But they can also root themselves in your mind, body, and energy field, which can create illnesses or negative, delayed reactions to situations since they've become rooted in your subconscious (like when your boss gets mad at you for showing up late to a meeting and you aren't given a chance to explain yourself but later pick a fight with your unassuming spouse when he or she forgets to load the dishwasher). A negative block plants a nasty seed that sprouts legs and kicks up all kinds of problems that you never saw coming.

Since feelings stem from beliefs, thoughts, and traumas—and are also energetic—I like to lean on them to tell me when my energy is light, bright, and high or vibrating on a lower and denser frequency. Low vibrational feelings create blocks after all, and blocks feel heavy. If a bill comes in the mail, you can choose to pay it and move on with neutral energy or freak out and lower your vibration. Since losing your mind feels awful, that's how you know that you're vibrating low and potentially creating a block. Pause for a moment. Is there anything in your life that's causing you to vibrate low or feel energetically heavy—maybe an e-mail from a co-worker, a date that you're nervous about, or a family conversation that you're dreading? Right now, choose to move on with neutral energy to keep from creating a block. How do you feel, once you do so?

You might also recognize a block when a situation stops working in your favor. Perhaps you're dating a new partner, and things begin to feel like they're at a standstill. This could make you feel confused or frustrated, which will lower energy and possibly cause a block. Trust me, I understand and have experienced these types of panics, and I know how rational it may seem at the time to default to a stressful response. But the moment you move toward neutrality, you'll reap a better emotional reward—and if you keep it up, you'll rebalance your response to all kinds of situations that come after it or are similar to it. We'll thoroughly explore a hierarchy of emotions as they relate to your vibration later in the book, but for now, know that it's easier to transition from a stressful state to a neutral one than it is to push yourself to be positive. It's a more realistic, emotional place to access within yourself.

So in future chapters, I'll show you how to use your feelings as a cue to get curious, minus the judgment, about why you feel the way you do so that you can immediately begin to feel better and raise your energy. Once you get to the root issue, you can address whether your programming is true, if it has to be true moving forward, and if not, what the new truth can be.

From a neuroscience perspective, the subconscious is always manifesting for you, and it has the potential to get in the way of what you hope to attain. But if you can figure out how it's working against your best interests and undo that process, you can rewire your mind so that all of your thoughts are on board with feeling that your goal is safe and what you deeply want. It's no secret that different thoughts trigger different brain reactions, but this happens so automatically that we don't even know it's occurring. The brain is doing what it's always been wired to do, and manifesting is often about getting the brain to stop going on autopilot in those neurological patterns and rewire itself to new pathways based on your ability to overhaul preconditioned thoughts and feelings. Once you've done this, it's suddenly so easy to manifest because you're not mentally or energetically combating all of your limiting beliefs. You must remove triggers and the past problems that you default to in a natural state of panic and anxiety, and then create a new pathway in the brain for your mind and energetic patterns to follow. From there, you'll change your behaviors and thoughts, and your goals will inadvertently come to fruition. And by the way, this can all happen quickly. The idea that we need to sit in therapy for 30 years to handle a trauma or belief is not always true. When I worked in a medical clinic in Norway, I witnessed my manifesting techniques outshine therapy. Today I watch it happen during the events that I hold all the time.

Fine-Tuning Your Subconscious

I have a secret psychological weapon—a concept I've coined "the subconscious reel," which is what every one of us is unconsciously telling ourselves, all day long, often based on our past programming. I call it a *reel* because it plays on a loop in your mind, over and over, until you choose to turn it off. This is where we do our most effective manifesting from, so again, if your subconscious thoughts are not pure and in your best interest, you will end up counter-manifesting your worst hopes and fears. You can spend an hour a day in meditation, reciting mantras, or journaling to create a small amount of change, if any at all, but if you have not purified your subconscious reel, you'll likely end up sabotaging your desires because a murky subconscious will have been firmly established at a profound level and be dictating the course of your life.

So let's say that you want to manifest a million dollars, but if you have unconscious trauma or false beliefs around wealth (perhaps you worry that having money will cause you to lose those you love, because it happened to a parent), no matter how often you consciously say that you want strong finances, you likely won't manifest a dime for yourself. Or, you will receive your desire but either quickly burn through it or lose it all in some other way because you're sending out energy from your subconscious that is in direct opposition of your conscious desires.

The initial stages of manifesting are about bringing the subconscious reel up to the conscious level so that it can be worked through. Many of us don't know which behaviors are holding us back or, as I have seen over the years, can be hidden in the oddest of places. The beautiful news is that if you become aware of these subconscious reels, it dissipates the energy and loosens the blockages, thus raising your vibration. Remember, your subconscious reel is powerful and can send out direct, oppositional energy to your conscious reel if the two are not aligned. You have to deal with the energy you're sending out, which stems from what's going on inside. When you get clear on the principles that define your authentic self, you become aligned with your true nature. Once you're in unison with your subconscious reel, your conscious reel helps create miraculous manifestations since the subconscious isn't sending it in the opposite direction. Instead, it's on board with a clear consciousness. I like to compare your consciousness to cells in the body. The more cells that are happy, healed, and acting in unison in the body, the healthier that body is. Similarly, the more we can create a unified energy, the faster we can manifest, and without repercussions like counter-manifesting or achieving only part of what we want.

Collectively, the eight practices will help align your subconscious and conscious reels to promote clear, conscious energy. What works against it are behaviors like complacency, an unwillingness to grow, and fear of change, as well as disempowering thoughts, beliefs, and actions, and continuing to choose the same dysfunction over and over. You have to be willing to release your white-knuckled grip on how you want your life to look based on past ideals, and have faith in growth and change. Believe it or not, a lot of us hold on to poor programming from our past. Though it's usually unconscious, it serves the need for protection and certainty. It's the devil you know, and it takes a concerted effort to break those patterns, but it's worth the effort because it feels amazing as it dissipates. When you willingly dig into your past, understand yourself, and change your programming . . . your energy automatically shifts, and manifestations quickly take hold.

What's God Got to Do with It?

The final component to influence your manifesting practice is various spiritual factors. These are the invisible forces that create manifestations that seem miraculous, unexpected, or like a "blessing." You don't need to go to church or have a specific faith to become a manifesting wiz, but you do need to believe in a higher power—whether you call this God, Universe, Source, what have you. This powerful outlet is the origin of all energy and embodies the highest good of all concerned.

I've found that upholding values like truth, love, authenticity, love, understanding, and love are essential to manifesting beautiful things (*love*, as you can tell, is most important of all!). These are high vibrational values, which I've been shown during countless channelings, will heal all things, including the worst past programming. They are powerful tools because when you use them, they can change your brain wiring and alter the manifestation process. Knowing good from bad, as it relates to your traumas and programming, also allows you to align yourself with the universe's greatest intentions for your future. Always acting with the highest good of all concerned in mind—which is to say, behaving in a way that most aligns with God's energy—is going to help keep you in stride with the highest values and vibrations of the universe as well.

One of the most important spiritual beliefs that I uphold is that God is always working for me. This means that whatever shows up for me is meant to teach me lessons for the highest good. Believing in the trust and guidance of a higher power allows me to stay in a higher vibrational state and helps me to better manifest without making it a selfish goal or creating resistance from my icky subconscious reel. When an upsetting event occurs, and it feels like the sky is falling, the goal is to always deal with it with a calm mood and neutral energy—and believing a higher power has your back will keep you there. This keeps you from vibrationally plummeting. In fact, let's try a test that proves as much. For the next 24 hours, trust that God is supporting you and that there's a purpose to all that occurs. For everything seemingly "bad" that happens *to* you, I'd like you to consider how this could be happening *for* you instead. How do you feel as these events occur, after they transpire, and once your daylong experiment is over? I'll bet making this mental shift automatically lightens your vibration since you're trusting in a divinely energetic plan rather than dropping into fear or a victim mentality. It should also make you feel empowered and open your mind to new possibilities for your future.

Most important of all, perhaps, is to remember that God's love isn't just unconditional love or infinite, high vibration; that energy is *instantaneous creation*. When we raise our vibration, we literally become part of The Greater Whole. And as we become close to Oneness with God through our programming and frequencies, we co-create what we want so much faster because we are a fractal of God who is the ultimate creator. God created all things and can continue to do so. God serves as a reminder of who we really are, at a soul level, even on this human plane.

Maintaining a solid, spiritual relationship with God, then, is important for partnering during the co-creation process but also with accessing your most authentic self. Our authenticity reflects who we are supposed to be, and it's who God created us to be. It's who we are at our most pure, soulful level. It reflects our essence without any preconceived notions or past programming. It is as close as we will get to Oneness with the universe on this plane of existence. I think back to when I began making spiritual videos for my Facebook page from my Florida apartment, which was the starting point for discovering who I really am and what I have to offer this world. There, I lived with no furniture, no friends, and no family close by. I slept on the floor, and my desk was an overturned cardboard box. And yet, I was outrageously happy. My relationship with God transformed too, which helped me feel supported and never alone. I realized, during this time, that God wasn't outside of me but part of me, and I felt more united with God than I could ever remember being. After clearing so many external influences from my life (like that abusive ex-boyfriend), I finally had the mental and spiritual space to intimately feel God's love, guidance, and presence. Ultimately, what God revealed to me during that time was *me*, in all my shining authenticity.

The clarity that came with this awakening led to countless breakthroughs. I channeled, I healed, and I journaled about my first future manifestations. I believe that we are all part of a larger existence, and as part of that limitless whole, if we try to be anything but authentic, it seems only natural that pain will find us. Life doesn't really work from that inauthentic space. But when we lean into the authentic version of ourselves, the universe's magic takes hold because we are now in flow with the way God created us and has orchestrated the universe to operate. If everyone on this planet tapped into their authentic selves, I believe this world would quickly heal and unify in ways we can only imagine.

I believe that co-creation, and thus manifestation, is integral to everyone's life path. The universe has given us the privilege of creating a life we want, here on earth, and that's a remarkable gift. Remember, as a fractal of God, that we get to experience co-creation with God, in the highest good of all, as we practice manifestation. And when we do it with authenticity and care for humanity, we're vastly rewarded, and everyone on the planet benefits in some way.

Tips and Takeaways

+ When creating a manifesting mindset, focus on the emotional state you'd like to have. Not the 3D "stuff" that you think will make you happy.

+ You're in charge of your world, you're here for a reason, and you can create what fulfills you.

+ Maintaining a relationship with God is important to the co--creation process.

+ Healing blocked energy is a must. This raises your vibration and lets you access abundant goals.

+ Past programming is made of beliefs, thoughts, and traumas that have shaped your worldview.

+ Past programming creates a high or low vibration and influences your manifesting outcomes.

✦ Your subconscious reel is what you unconsciously tell yourself, all day long, based on past programming. Becoming aware of this dissipates the energy, loosens energetic blockages, and raises your vibration. Once you're united with your subconscious reel, manifestations occur.

More Resources and Free Downloads

If you enjoyed this chapter, I've put together a simple one-page downloadable sheet called *"17 Ways to Raise Your Vibration"* that reveals simple, easy, and predictable ways to raise your personal vibration so you can manifest what you want faster. Download it for free at www.authenticliving.com/gifts

Chapter 3

THE SCIENCE
OF MANIFESTING

Imagine that you're peacefully working away on your laptop in your favorite coffee shop, sipping your morning latte, and catching up on e-mails when a stranger sits down at the table next to you. You don't talk or even acknowledge each other's presence, so this person certainly does nothing to noticeably alarm you, and yet their mere existence gives you a weird feeling that you just can't shake. You try to ignore the sensation, but it won't go away. Your stomach feels uneasy, your neck and shoulders stiffen, and there's just something about the stranger that doesn't quite feel right.

What you're experiencing isn't a burst of psychic ability or evidence that you're losing your grip on reality; it's the physical presentation of how it feels when a person's energy interacts with yours, and in this case, is not harmonious. The result is a very real and tangible reaction. Every one of us is able to sense energy to differing extents, be it positive or negative, and this can happen when we are in the presence of one or many living or nonliving entities. You can just as easily feel joyful and uplifted as you can feel creeped out or repelled by surrounding energy waves. Think about how effortlessly your mood shifts when you're feeling down but then bump into a happy friend who instantly cheers you up. We like to say that their sunny attitude "rubs off" on us, but what's really happening is that their energy influences ours in the best of ways.

These familiar examples demonstrate that energy isn't something that's outside of us but inside of us too; that we're constantly interacting with energy, in some way, shape, or form, to help us intuitively understand our surroundings. This "energetic soup" that we're all swimming in—which typically can't be seen but is easily felt—creates both our behavior and reality every single day. Our ability to sense, and make sense of, what we feel when we encounter energy is meant to help us quickly and effortlessly recognize whether we're in situations that are good or bad for us and either raise or lower our vibrations as a result. Remember, in order to co-create our reality, we need to exist in as high of a vibrational state as we can; God doesn't want us to spend time with other people, or in situations, that emotionally deplete us or keep us stuck in a vibe that makes it difficult to excel, achieve, and manifest all that we desire. Surrounding ourselves with energy that's compatible with our own can make or break relationships, careers, finances, health, and other important priorities that determine whether we thrive on earth.

As an energetic being, you react to both animate and inanimate objects as well as countless other things including conversations, thoughts, emotions, traumas, organs in your body, and even diseases. When you die and no longer have a physical state, your energetic presence continues to exist in the universe, given that the first law of thermodynamics says that energy cannot be created or destroyed. Energy is, however, always conserved and can be converted from one form to another. Throughout time, your energy has always mingled with the energy around it, in various configurations, to help create the whole of existence. It always will.

In this chapter, I'm going to share the scientific information I've learned while working with academics and clinicians, studying metaphysics on my own, and channeling from divine sources during meditation—all, as they relate to supporting the eight secrets in Part II. I came to much of this information when I was in my early 20s, and then years later, when I partnered with renowned scientists in a health clinic in Norway. In this setting and other clinical environments, I worked alongside doctors, psychiatric nurses, scientists, and researchers to help heal issues involving the heart, liver, digestive system, nervous system, and immune system from tough psychosomatic health cases that traditional doctors couldn't seem to crack on their own. It was a real eye-opening experience, to say the least.

And while I've been gathering scientific data for years, my mind and consciousness rarely spit it back out in a literal sense. Instead, when I teach these fascinating insights to clients and at workshops, the universe often guides me to channel and marry ideas in a way you may have never heard before. I am not a scientist or doctor, but what I present here is some of the science that the universe tells me is related to how manifestation works when you use the eight secrets. Because many of the details about energy, brain wiring, psychology, and how these impact and change our lives can become quite complicated when you extrapolate them out even further, I will only share what is necessary to digest my manifesting techniques, then suggest we move on to practicing them. After all, you'll feel the magic when your life transforms before your very eyes!

Let's Talk Auras

So we all have an auric field. Here, biological circuits carry electrical currents through a complex wiring system that lives in your body although these currents are generated on multiple layers outside of it. Together, this creates an electromagnetic field that surrounds your physical body and extends at least 18 inches outward, which is what we call an aura.

All matter radiates an auric field. Even inanimate objects like rocks and apples have auric fields, though they are not as extensive as that of living organisms. It's believed that you have seven bands in your auric fields that connect your physical body to your spiritual body, where all of your experiences, memories, and emotions are held. Your auric field is also connected to your chakra system, which has been compared to a spiritual nervous system that runs along your spine. The word *chakra* translates to "wheel" or "disk" in Sanskrit and refers to the energy centers in your body. These wheels or disks of spinning energy each correspond to certain nerve bundles and major organs. When your chakras are open and balanced, energy runs through them, and your body, mind, and spirit are in harmony. Imagine them, at their best, as spinning wheels of free-flowing, positive energy. In the body, your chakras begin at the base of your spine and extend up to the crown of your head. From top to bottom, your chakras are your crown, third eye, throat, heart, solar plexus, sacral, and root chakra.

Your auric field is always changing based on your health and well-being as well as the energy with which you constantly come in contact. You are always processing data and information in your mind, and I like to think of our energy field receiving similar information as well. Your field affects your physical, emotional, and spiritual bodies and influences whether you radiate a larger, brighter, more productive, and higher vibration or a minimal, dim, and weak aura and vibration. The stronger your aura, the less affected you are by the low energy of those around you. And with balanced chakras and a bright, clean aura, you have the ability to bring peace and calm to others with your presence alone. I equate having a healthy field and chakras to having healthy cells in your body. If cells are healthy, they can communicate properly, and thus positively impact your body. And if a person is energetically healthy, they not only can impact their own energy and physical body, but others' too. The latter is so important because if we can influence one another's energy by keeping our vibrations high and strong, then we'll always be surrounded by humans whose collective energy can help sustain ours. Those who work to change their vibration and strengthen their aura always make a grand difference in the world.

Chances are you've tried to deliberately influence another person's field—like when you try to cheer up a grumpy friend—but have never realized that this is what you're doing. As a fun experiment, choose a person who's in a bad or sad mood, and attempt to shift their aura with yours. Devote 20 minutes to this three-step process. First, while you're together, assess how you think the person feels. Then consider how *you* feel and sense the difference between your two energies. Finally, send that person love with either kind words or by envisioning them wrapped in a bubble shaped like a pink or gold heart. All the while, your disposition should feel helpful, loving, and grounded. Don't escalate the other person's mood; attempt to neutralize or boost it. If all goes according to plan, your mutual, high vibrations will support each other's in the best way.

Info In, Info Out

I like to think of the auric field as your body's filtration and communication systems. When your auric field first encounters another source's energy, it needs to decide what to do with it. And once the two energies make contact, the incoming energy doesn't remain the same in your field. This is similar to what happens if you drop a pebble into a still pond, and its impact causes the water to ripple outward. Now imagine that someone on the other side of the pond drops a pebble that creates a second ripple. Once these two ripples meet, they change how they're moving, and the ripples look different, right? This is similar to what happens when your energy waves encounter frequencies from an outside source; these vibrations affect yours and create a new kind of merged frequency. This new frequency then goes through a process that reminds me of filtration, and it determines whether this joined energy brings you down or lifts your vibration up. If the wave dampens your energy, you might feel mentally cloudy or stressed out, and it can even begin to create a block, like we talked about in Chapter 2. On the other hand, your filter can also welcome or elevate the energy that it receives, which is a process called "transmuting." It's easier for a positive wave to raise your spirits and combat any negative energy than it is for negative energy to break down an existing high vibration because positive energy is so strong. Just as a pin prick of light can illuminate a room full of darkness, so can your bright and powerful field.

Your eventual goal isn't to reach a state where you spend your whole day dodging negative energy so you can keep your vibration high; this would mean editing your life down to a bubble, surrounded only by upbeat people and situations, which isn't realistic. You also can't minimize the energetic frequencies you encounter unless you want to isolate yourself. Instead, your aim is to learn how to manage your frequency in an elevated state, regardless of who or what is interacting with it. You want your energy field to be resilient to stress so you can live in the real world, in such a high vibrational state that most things can't touch you. To be honest, when you're in a high state, it's rare that those in lower states can co-exist with you anyway; they tend to be repelled. You end up inadvertently paring down your social and professional worlds unless the people in them choose to elevate with you. When this happens, it reminds me of how you can use a charged battery to wake up a dead one because the charged one gives it juice.

As I was learning how to sustain my high vibration during those early days of channeling and practicing the eight secrets, I had a close childhood friend whose voice alone could send my mood plummeting. I'd panic every time she called because I'd feel obligated to talk to her due to an unhealed need in me to please people. She'd constantly talk about everything that was wrong with her life, and we'd usually end the call with either an awkward silence or outright argument if I offered a different perspective than hers. However, my friend and I had history, and I loved her. I also knew that I only saw one version of her, and she'd grown used to a version of me that was once negative too, so sometimes I'd unconsciously mirror her low vibes so that we'd feel connected. I knew this was unhealthy, and I wanted to figure out a way to keep her around without us rubbing off on each other in a bad way. I also wanted to remove low vibrational behaviors from my life so that I could show her that a happier life was possible for her too.

I decided to work on what I could control—which was raising my vibration, particularly focusing on the exercises you'll learn in Chapter 5, when we detangle your dense energy. Over the course of three months, I had a fresh perspective on our relationship. It felt as if I were wearing a new pair of glasses when we were together because I saw things so differently! I had compassion, patience, boundaries—and my higher vibration helped me to naturally default to the positive mental spaces that helped me deal with my friend's lower vibe. I didn't jump into her negativity or feel impacted by it. I had empathy for her and saw that she needed love, not judgment. My aura's filter now took what my friend threw at me and separated it from my energy so it didn't harm me. It felt like I'd installed a sheet of plexiglass between us. I saw her behavior for what it was, but at a distance and in a way that didn't affect me anymore. This let us build a new and more authentic relationship, and I didn't have to abandon her to feel at peace.

While your aura's filtration system is powerful, its communication system is equally complex, as your energetic field uses your body like an antenna to receive data and then send it to your brain, which deciphers it. Because antennas can receive and send out information, you then send a frequency back out to the world, as we've discussed. Your auric field and antenna allow your energy to interact in harmonious or disharmonious ways with others' energy. Our brains are always receiving different frequencies and energies—from family, friends, fellow commuters, the foods we eat, electronics in our home, plants, and so on—that change both our personal and collective vibrations. Innumerable frequencies are everywhere, as our brains store and process a lot of information each day. For instance, during our leisure time, each one of us can process 34 gigabytes or 100,000 words alone every day! Think about how these words make up your thoughts, which carry energy waves, and how your body has to then do something with these vibes—access, store, or get rid of them. It's a lot of work, and very collaborative at that!

Though your auric field has many different frequencies, it does have a dominant frequency that develops over the years. To put it simply, this is the percentage of time that you are dominantly positive or negative with a relative amount of consistency, and it is often based on programming (before you learn or apply the eight secrets from this book, of course!). Your energy is mostly based on your abundance of thoughts, so what's going on in your mind is what determines your dominant frequency. When your frequency is high and in alignment with the universe, then instantaneous manifestations can occur. You have the ability to process information, you are in a state of clarity, and you're in flow with the universe for good things to transpire. If you're in a dominantly high vibe state, this will also positively impact others and then come back to you, like a boomerang.

Curious about your own dominant frequency? Let's try an activity to figure it out. On a sheet of paper, write down the major categories in your life that are most important to you: for example, family, friends, love, money, abundance, career, relationship with self, and overall fulfillment. Now consider whether you are satisfied with each one and answer *yes*, *no*, or *maybe* next to each category. Remember, this isn't about whether you're excelling in these areas, but how they make you *feel*. The number of yeses and noes on the page indicates how high or low your dominant frequency may be. No matter what your ranking is now, I promise that your dominant frequency will be higher as you improve your practices by the end of the book.

Creating a positive dominant frequency is one reason it's so important to sift through your past programming and related thoughts before diving into the eight secrets. It's perfectly normal to experience a range of emotions in your day, but if you do feel a negative impulse coming on, you'll simply frame it as energetic feedback, instead of assigning a discouraging meaning to it. Energy is always oscillating in and around you, so what you're feeling is really just a moment in time and a wave of energy that hit you but can easily just float on by like a cloud instead of attaching to your thoughts and amplifying them. This mindset creates mental distance to help you process the trigger, understand it, and move on quickly.

So how does your auric field affect the tangible and emotional life that you want to manifest? Since all things are energy, your field impacts the atoms and particles around you. As many quantum physics studies have shown, atoms move in certain ways, based on intention. Many channelings and private experiments have also shown that if the observer expects particles to do something, they will do it, based on the suppositions and energy that the observer sends out. This is what decides the behavior of the particles. How fascinating is that? What we expect to happen most will occur because of our expectations that are driven by thought energy. This is such an automatic process that it's hard to recognize it in our behaviors because we don't realize how fast energy can travel from our minds. But we are all connected, and those atomic particles are reacting to the higher energy form which is the observer. They move and vibrate in the way that is expected of them. If you can keep yourself in a high vibrational state and have strong intentions for the good of all when you manifest the future, this helps desires come to fruition. Thoughts become things, very quickly and easily, because your thoughts and field are aligned.

Train Your Brain to Manifest

As I mentioned earlier, our brains fire and wire in relation to the energy in and around us to create our behavior and reality. Our brains are also wired, according to our past programming, in a way that allows consistent, neurological pathways to send information via electricity. If you have a thought or experience, these create wave frequencies, and at the same time, from a psychology perspective, these thoughts and experiences will cue you to tell yourself what they mean. The meanings you place on these thoughts are most often based on prewired neurological pathways that have been carved over years of conditioning yourself to think the same way, and usually on cue from a trigger. So when certain stimuli is presented to your mind and auric field, the brain energetically and mentally fires the same way over and over again.

The practices you'll learn in this book will interrupt this repeat firing and replace old thoughts with new ones, which will help create new neurological pathways in the brain. Your new thoughts will carry a high vibration, so when you are ready to manifest, you will not be held back by past programming or the low energy that comes with it. Not only that, but your natural reactions to people, events, and even your own momentary thoughts will now default to a more empowered state that helps you maintain your high vibration. This improved, energetic frequency is one that the universe immediately recognizes and wants to match, which will help your desires manifest in a faster way. I have seen this phenomenon occur countless times, but it never gets old to hear a client exclaim that after training her brain to exhibit less anxiety, fear, and fewer disempowering beliefs that she can suddenly manifest her goals and optimal feelings at breakneck speed. I can almost see the fresh electricity zipping around, in new and intricate patterns, inside her head!

Because the brain is responsible for so much energetic messaging, you can see why working through and then replacing your past programming and its related frequencies are so essential. If you send out positive or negative thoughts, whether they're conscious or unconscious, that is what you will get back, and it becomes reinforced in your neurological wiring (this premise operates similarly to what some refer to as the law of attraction, but I like to view it from a more clinical perspective). Your ability to rewire your brain falls under the umbrella of neuroplasticity, or brain plasticity, which is the ability of the brain's neural networks to change through growth, learning, experiences, and reorganization. These modifications can range from individual neuron pathways forming new connections to more systematic changes like cortical remapping. In fact, the natural concept known as brain pruning removes connections in the brain that are no longer needed and strengthens those that are frequently used. So if you build a new habit, say through one or more of the eight secrets, you will build a new pathway to support it, which becomes more rewarding over time. I lean on brain pruning and neuroplasticity a lot when I teach manifesting.

If a client, for instance, tells me she feels unworthy of love, then we work to disrupt the neurological pathway that isn't serving her, and we do this so strongly that she creates new pathways that establish a foundation for higher vibrations, better energetic output, and positive manifestations. Years ago, at an event, a woman announced to the group that she didn't feel she was good enough to pursue her purpose work, which she felt was to help others, because she had a daughter who was battling a tragic past event. The daughter had been molested, and this mother felt that she should've somehow protected her child and was self-flagellating as a result.

We got to the root of the mom's problem, which was a belief that wasn't true—that she needed to punish herself. I referred to this as her "currency" because it was how she paid for what she felt she'd done wrong. Behind all our negative beliefs is a currency that we dole out; some might pay by not being abundant or by developing health problems. This woman paid with self-loathing. Within a few hours and after a series of exercises, this mom realized that it was okay if she felt unhappy from time to time, but she couldn't keep paying for what she did to the extent that it kept her from serving others. She decided that she needed to go from feeling unworthy and needing to struggle to declaring that it is precisely *because* her daughter suffered, she had to help others. She reframed her perspective and created an accountability system that included peer support and daily exercises to reinforce the new neural pathways she'd formed that day. A few months later, she became certified as a Love and Authenticity Practitioner with our company and is doing the work that she feels her soul was created to do—with no guilt, only love and beautiful intentions. Her new mindset has also allowed her to be more helpful to her daughter too, because she listens and supports her from a foundation of love rather than guilt.

If thoughts become things, then the *right* thoughts create pathways that fire in healthy ways, and those become your natural default when a situation throws you off. These new and improved pathways send out positive, high vibrations that we then send out to the world. It's the difference between emitting a low vibration formed by a brain that's been wired to think *How can this go wrong, and what's my problem?* to flipping it around to become one that's been rewired in the brain to automatically think *What can go right, and how can I improve?*

Growth and brain plasticity can be at their most powerful when you visually surround yourself with behaviors that are positive. This is because mirror neurons in the brain are activated when you perform a task and when you watch someone else performing a task. However, these mirror neurons are only activated if you watch an action that you can perform yourself (for instance, they're not activated if you look at a bird flying). These neurons also light up when you imagine an action that you can do but aren't at the time. Mirror neurons contribute to why you can sometimes feel what others feel, like if you're watching a movie and an actor gets stabbed, you might wince when he's impaled as if you can feel his pain. For the rest of the day, notice how often you react as if you are doing a certain activity though you will be simply watching someone else participate in it—perhaps your stomach will drop when your child jumps off a diving board or your mouth will water when a friend bites into a juicy apple. Because the brain is not a rigid network of neurons and is always trying to find better ways to manage and deliver information by creating or removing neural connections, the act of watching others behave the way that you want tells your mirror neurons that you are acting that way too, which can create and reinforce new neural pathways. This will further encourage your brain to eliminate old negative feedback and establish new connections.

My mom always told me, "If you're the smartest person in the room, then you're in the wrong room." She was so right! In other words—and especially for your manifesting purposes—be sure to always surround yourself with those you can learn from and want to be like so that your brain can wire similarly to theirs. If our brains are wired to look for solutions, positivity, inspiration, and love, then we show up in the world as such. We vibrate at a higher frequency, and our bodies that double as electrical antennas send out frequencies that the universe can respond to. When we vibrate high, we can manifest faster and with objectives aligned with our highest and most authentic self.

The Proof Is in the Pudding

When I worked in health clinics throughout Scandinavia, I studied the psychosomatic root of many illnesses and helped a lot of patients get well by using various exercises and practices, some of which I include in this book. But more than anything, watching patients suffer so dramatically from what turned out to be illnesses rooted in negative thoughts or experiences—and then helping them recover with energetic practices that were not driven by meds or other traditional medical techniques—deeply built and reinforced so many of my theories about manifestation. When studying diseases that occurred when emotional states expressed themselves in the body, I realized that if thought energy could tell the heart to shut down or create disharmony in a patient's liver cells—if you and I could do something that manipulative to matter as dense as our bodies—then we should be able to affect other realities that haven't occurred yet, like our job or purpose work. *Boom!* This metaphor cracked open my understanding of how powerful the brain is and how it's wired to behave when we have less than optimal thoughts and vibrations. These can either reimagine a perfectly healthy body or feed the creation of disease that might have a physiological root like an infection or genetic quirk but tip that condition into an illness more pervasive and harmful.

One of the most fascinating stories I can recall is about a set of twin brothers that I worked with at the Norway clinic. Together, they came in with various allergies and inexplicable reactions to their environments (incidentally, 90 percent of allergies that we studied turned out to be psychosomatic). Though there was a lot of overlap in the twins' various conditions, one of the men had a severe bee allergy that caused him to go into anaphylactic shock when he was stung while the other man did not have an allergy to bees at all. After working with both patients, we discovered that when the brothers were four years old and playing together in the woods one day, they encountered a beehive, stepped on it, and were swarmed by the vengeful insects. One of the boys ran back to the house and was comforted by his mom; he felt safe and recovered fine from his stings. The other boy ran farther into the woods, got lost, was found alone hours later, and experienced a great deal of trauma around this event. As it turns out, the child who felt safe at home did not grow up to be allergic to bees, but the one who felt fearful and alone in the woods had the severe allergy.

So, I worked with the allergic man to help him understand that feeling a lack of safety was at the root of his psychosomatic illness/allergy, and we dismantled the reinforcing beliefs that he'd told himself around this incident too. I also helped him recognize how the safety theme was showing up in his life as an adult, and from there, helped desensitize him through a series of conversations and a therapeutic device we used called an eductor, which essentially combines bioresonance therapy (this measures the frequency of energy wavelengths coming from the body) and biofeedback (this uses various types of feedback to gain control over involuntary bodily functions like blood flow, blood pressure, and heart rate).

The result was miraculous. Within a few sessions, I learned that this man's allergy was greatly desensitized.

What's so interesting to me about my studies is that with each patient, there was no consistent cause and reaction—in other words, mom issues didn't always create heart problems. This is because our neurological pathways are so intricate and specific to our individual programming. Even so, I was able to play a role in patients rewiring their minds to stop telling their bodies to hurt themselves; I helped them disrupt their programming and thoughts, and thus changed their neuropathways to send out higher electrical impulses, in an improved auric field, which set the stage for manifesting good health and a happier life in general. Most of us don't know which of our thoughts cause disharmony, much less how to change them without some guidance. These are often automatic responses that are so hardwired that it takes a concerted effort to change them. This is why the best manifesters have the eight secrets ingrained in their minds and auric fields. The more these tenets become part of who you are and how you walk through your days, the easier it becomes to bring your deepest and healthiest desires to life.

Tips and Takeaways

✦ Energy is everywhere. You constantly interact with it to intuitively "read" your environment.

✦ The energy around you and how you process it affects your physical, emotional, and spiritual bodies and influences the kind of aura you radiate.

✦ Surround yourself with people who have the energy you'd like to have; they will help you sustain your own vibration too.

✦ Though your auric field has many different frequencies, it has a dominant frequency that develops over the years. This is based on how often you are dominantly positive or negative.

✦ You want your energy field to be resilient to stress so that you can live in the real world but in such a high vibrational state that most things can't touch you.

✦ Your brain fires and wires relative to the energy in and around you. The eight secrets interrupt negative firing and replace old thoughts with new ones; this creates new pathways in the brain.

✦ When your brain is wired to look for solutions, positivity, inspiration, and love, then you show up in the world as such. You vibrate at a higher frequency, and your body doubles as an electrical antenna that sends out frequencies that the universe can positively respond to. When you vibrate high, you can manifest faster and in alignment with your most authentic self.

More Resources and Free Downloads

If you enjoyed this chapter, I've put together a downloadable pdf called "The ULTIMATE Guide to Your Chakras and Aura" that reveals the different kinds of chakras (even the hidden ones), how to tell if they are blocked, and what you can do right now to unblock them. Download it for free at www.authenticliving.com/gifts

Part II

The
8 SECRETS
of
POWERFUL
MANIFESTERS

Chapter 4

Secret #1

CREATE ENERGETIC CHECK-INS

So the first practice of powerful manifesters is actually a two-
-stepper: 1) become aware of your emotional and energetic states
so that you can 2) start to elevate your vibration to a more positive
level. And you do all of this by conducting energetic check-ins at
regular intervals throughout the day. Now you're not going to work
through all of your past programming in this first practice so that
your energy instantly accelerates to its highest vibration possible,
but you will begin to recognize how your dominant thoughts and
feelings cause you to have the experiences you do. (The beauty of
the eight secrets is that each one builds on the last, though you will
benefit from them individually too.) From there, thanks to the work
that we do together in future chapters, you'll be able to clearly comb
through your influential thoughts and emotions and establish a
foundation that's optimal for manifesting with ease and precision.

Energetic check-ins are so key because they teach you to become highly aware of the beliefs that inform your thoughts, which impact your vibration and ability to manifest. Though you will initially make a concerted effort to check in a few times a day, check-ins will soon become habit; in my experience, check-ins can take from two weeks to three months to become instinctual. At its simplest, this important first secret helps you to become really conscious of your emotional highs and lows throughout the day so that you can elevate to higher states of centeredness and with more consistency, which is at the heart of manifesting your very best life.

When you frequently check in with how you're feeling, you can also affect your emotions at any time and thus, regulate your corresponding energy at any time. Remember, when your body and energy field receive an energy frequency, they turn it into a thought that creates certain emotions. Once your brain processes this information, it sends out new signals, which cause an energetic frequency to be outwardly emitted from you. This elicits a response in your environment and vibrational fields. Energetic frequencies are like waves that rise and drop all day, every day, and when they do, our brains pour a ton of energy into their corresponding feelings— and it's these feelings that determine your dominant and consistent frequency, which sets the stage for manifesting conscious or unconscious desires. No wonder powerful manifesters stay aware of their emotional state at all times; they know they have the ability to create a dominant energy field that can bring about what they want, faster and more easily.

The simplest and most consistent means of enforcing regular check-ins is to schedule these hits of self-reflection and commit to addressing whatever feelings and topics they push to the surface of your mind. Once you know what's going on deep down inside you, you'll be ready to address the factors that hold you back and do the work to remove them. To put it another way, what you're doing here is bringing the subconscious reel to the conscious level so you can remove its sticking points and blocks; in no time, this will become as easy as breathing, and massively beneficial too. In this chapter, I'll teach you how to check in with yourself, suggest questions and exercises to acknowledge what's going on, and encourage you to continue this method until check-ins are your new norm. With practice, your brain and energetic field will begin to align with your highest self and the universe's generosity. You'll develop a hyperawareness about how you live, or living consciously. Once you're comfortable doing check-ins, you'll move on to the next secret, where you'll dig into the deeper work of untangling the dense energy and programming that you discover during check-in sessions.

Beep-Beep-Beep! Time to Check In!

Set an alarm on your phone, Alexa, or in a central location in your home to go off three times a day: first thing in the morning when you wake up, around noon or midday, and at night before you go to bed. When the alarm goes off, you're going to ask yourself a series of six simple questions that I list in the box on the following page. You will continue to do daily check-ins for 15 days, and then graduate to hourly check-ins for an eight-hour window for the next 15 days. After that, I find that check-ins become instinctual, and you won't need to set an alarm. You will check in with yourself as feelings arise.

As you move through the check-in questions, the energy behind this practice should be one of cool curiosity and then awareness, not obsessiveness or inner conflict. Your goal is to embrace this process as one that lends itself to growth and improvement, which is exciting and fun! These kinds of thoughts will help elicit a positive feeling and light vibe—not a neurotic or overly methodical one. If at any point, you find yourself feeling anxious or stressed out during check-ins, you can try one or more grounding exercises. Keep them in the back of your mind because when you're new to this process, you might feel overwhelmed as you begin to touch on the beliefs that define you, no matter how hard you try to view them through the lens of a detached and curious observer. The best grounding exercises interrupt and elevate your thoughts and emotions. They can also double as pattern interrupts, so you can use them for that purpose as well.

I had a client who found immediate relief by grounding herself doing jumping jacks while shouting, "I'm a star!" This made her laugh, which helped break the tension she initially felt during her check-ins. Other grounding exercises include saying a quick prayer or taking a few deep breaths with your hand over your heart. Another grounding option is to envision someone you admire (I used to use Oprah) clapping their hands in front of your face, as if to say, "Not today, kiddo! Snap out of it!" My favorite exercise, though, is turning your thoughts into animated cartoons. Recalling a frustrating conversation with Mom isn't so upsetting when she's dressed like a Disney princess.

The Big Six

The following are six check-in questions to ask yourself each time your alarm does its thing. You don't need to commit these to memory, but do jot them down on a sticky note or in a journal so they're accessible. Thanks to the repetition of this exercise, you'll memorize them in no time.

1. How do I feel right now? Rate your emotional state on a scale from 1 to 10.

2. Why am I feeling this way?

3. Am I reliving the past?

4. Am I worried about the future?

5. What do I think is going to happen?

6. Is this even mine?

Now let's explore these questions individually so that you can understand how to approach each one and what role they might play in your larger manifestation goals. You may want to record your answers in a journal to track your changes and improvement. But this isn't necessary to do. You may just prefer to keep a mental log, and that's fine too.

You May Ask Yourself . . .

Question #1: How Do I Feel Right Now?

The first and most important question that you can ask yourself is *How do I feel right now?* The moment you do, pay attention to your immediate response, which could land anywhere on the positive-to-negative spectrum. Do your mind and body answer with a physical feeling, an emotional one, an energetic response—or some combination? Physical feelings present in the body, say as butterflies, loose or tense muscles, a headache or stomachache, or even a physical tic. Emotional responses stem from the mind, and might include happiness, silliness, shame, and depression. Those are easy enough to identify since we're used to feeling them all the time.

Then we have energetic feelings, which are harder to detect, especially during your initial check-ins. It takes practice to recognize how you're interacting with the energy around you. To me, positive, energetic feelings create an energized, electric sensation around my physical body, along with a lightness in the air around me; more negative ones feel heavy and thick, almost like a dense fog. What might be more helpful to notice at first is how the energy in your environment is interacting with your field by recognizing anything unusual that's occurring in your midst. You'll know this is happening because as soon as you ask your brain a question, it tries to answer either mentally or environmentally as the universe works in unison by sending you "signs" that reflect the answers to those questions. For instance, you might ask yourself how you're feeling, and if the sensation is a negative one, later you might also spill your tea, stub your toe, find that a contract gets stalled, or like me, have an amethyst crystal randomly fall on your head from the high ledge of a bookshelf! If it's positive, you might notice an increased number of situations and relationships falling into place. The more you live in an elevated vibrational state, the more these signs will happen. The process of creating signs starts with God, but because you co-create with God, they eventually manifest because of how God's energy merges with yours.

It's important to become attuned to all types of feelings because negative and positive energies impact us very differently. I believe that when negative energies strike, they begin with energetic imprints, then manifest in the emotional body, and if you don't deal with those emotions, they manifest in the physical body as illness. This is one of the reasons why you want to get ahead of these feelings and manage them, before they cause problems that require more effort to resolve than if you simply check in with yourself throughout the day. What's great is that when your feelings are positive, they also have the ability to build and amplify, depending on how much energy you pour into them. So if you wake up feeling peppy or optimistic after lunch, stop what you're doing and make it a point to memorize what that emotional state really feels like in your mind, body, and even energetic field if you can. Eventually, you'll find ways to match and even exceed these sensations, which indicate that you're in flow with an elevated frequency.

Since emotions not only motivate what we consciously and unconsciously think and do but influence our vibrations that make manifesting happen, I'd like you to start viewing them only as objective feedback. That's all: they're just your response to a situation that's neither positive nor negative and is little more than data right now. So if you feel anxious or grumpy, do not catastrophize this; and if you feel a good emotion, don't overthink that either. You are going to return to this feedback during subsequent check-in questions and later in the book.

Now that you're aware of what you feel, consider whether these are acute or chronic emotions. Taking this into account is so essential, because it readies your mind for evaluating the emotion's root cause. It's also helpful to know that acute feelings are easier to deal with while they're still in their infancy than with chronic ones, but if you don't address them, they can actually compound with other feelings and blocked energies, and become a complicated, ongoing mess. So if you immediately notice that how you feel is carried over from an argument you had last night with your dad, then it's safe to assume that this is an acute feeling. However, if you notice that what you feel is familiar, and perhaps it's the same way you've woken up every day this week or this month, then it may be triggered by a chronic situation that you get to address.

Finally, rate how you feel on a scale from 1 to 10. If you're logging your progress in a journal, you may want to compare how you rank now to how you ranked in the past. This will help you to chart your progress and recognize in real time how your emotional picture shifts and improves and how those improvements can lead to a life that magically falls into place.

Question #2: Why Am I Feeling This Way?

Now that you've connected with how you feel, let's explore what situation (or situations) those feelings are attached to. This question cues the subconscious reel to begin rising to the conscious mind so that we can start examining the limiting beliefs that are creating the thoughts that hamper high vibrations and get in the way of positive manifestations. For instance, if your subconscious is rooted in fear, as most people's limiting beliefs and subsequent thoughts are, then conscious manifestation will be impossible in this heavy state. So when you wake up with a knot in your stomach and realize that it's because you're upset about a recent breakup, this will bring that story to the conscious level so that you can take steps to dissolve related worries until they're no longer an issue.

On the other hand, if your feelings are attached to a positive situation, then this is a good thing! Here, you're vibing on a positive frequency, and again, your job is to get familiar with how that feels and then recognize it when you're in similar situations so you can sustain or even elevate this feeling/frequency as often as possible. For example, if you notice how fulfilled and happy you feel after a walk or when you're playing with your cute grandchild, then not only should you do this more often but this is the frequency you should seek to match from other activities and companions. The more you re-create the frequency signature of these activities, the more often your energy will exist on this vibration and pull in other opportunities that match this intentional energy. Before you know it, you and this high vibration become one.

The answer to why you feel the way you do might be obvious or more complicated. You may be happy about something as simple as a conversation you had with a loved one or a funny show you watched on TV. Or, if you feel badly, you could be worried about money, your kids, job, marriage, or all of the above. When most people check in and find that they have negative feelings, they often don't know why they're upset and need to consciously explore this. Over the years I've learned that if you can't immediately figure out why you're out of sorts, then this can mean that your brain doesn't want to face the answer (if someone says to me, "I don't know why I'm upset," this tells me that there's a buried issue just waiting to be uprooted). Your psyche already thinks there isn't a solution to a buried problem or that finding one will bring up too much pain or too many uncomfortable emotions. You might also subconsciously worry that you'll have to relive the trauma in order to heal. In short, your psyche will always make an effort to protect you, but the truth is staying hidden from your traumas is little more than sabotage.

The good news is that you don't have to dig that deep for that long to recognize which beliefs impair your thoughts and then obstruct your ability to positively manifest. You don't have to spend years in therapy or constantly sift through the ins and outs of your trauma. You just have to get to the belief that was created by the situation at hand, which we'll do in the next chapter. From being in abusive relationships, I created a belief that I'd always be used by other people and that men aren't very nice. My reality then began to show up as such because I was living and dying by that belief. And if I were to obsessively pick at the trauma until it became my identity, I'd keep myself in a low vibrational state. It's always important to examine the thoughts that feed the beliefs around your trauma so that you can dismantle them. But the energy behind this intention should remain thoughtful, clear, and levelheaded. To properly heal the beliefs that will impact your manifestations, you'll need to peel back enough layers to help you work through the past programming that hinders your subconscious reel—and determine if your beliefs are even true. (Spoiler alert: they rarely are.)

Question #3: **Am I Reliving the Past?**

Once you identify the situation that's causing your feelings, notice if it happened in the past—and if the way that you feel is keeping you rooted there. So often we allow what happened days, months, or years ago to control how we feel in the now, but this isn't real life. When you live in the past, you are either trying to re-create it or run as far from it, as fast as you can. This can happen with deep issues, like when you try to revive an old romance after it's run its course or avoid trauma by dodging situations that feel similar to one that caused you pain. It can also happen with mundane, daily events. I'll never forget how, back in college, I gave a big presentation to my business class—and let's just say, it wasn't my best work. I was full of anxiety leading up to the talk, terrified during it, and slunk back to my seat as if I spoke gibberish for 20 minutes. Though I did well enough to earn a good grade, this experience ruined public speaking for me for a long time. For years as an adult, I shied away from large events where I was front and center—no matter how great the opportunity or pay—because I couldn't shake the past. I was convinced that every engagement would go down just like my class presentation and leave me feeling ashamed and vulnerable. It took concerted work to dismantle this belief and the thoughts that stemmed from it before I could engage large groups again. Today, I have little issue with public speaking because I can see that what happened in the past has no true bearing on what is happening, and could potentially occur, in the now.

The obvious problem with reliving the past is that whether you are hanging on to a negative or positive memory, you are missing out on all of the wonderful (or at least, neutral!) emotions and experiences available to you in the world right now. You may also be keeping yourself stuck in a bad scenario or stagnant energy cycle because you're constantly manifesting from a past experience and the stagnant vibrational energy that's attached to it. What's more, your head is what lives in the past (and the future), but your heart can only live in the present. I've found that the most impressive manifestations come from the heart space and are lubricated by the energetic frequency of love, which we'll explore in later chapters.

Question #4: Am I Worried about the Future?

Just as your feelings might be rooted in the past, it's also common to cling to worrisome future scenarios outside your current reality. When you do this, you don't deal with what is happening in the moment. Your thoughts and all their energy feed a scenario that might not even occur. You likely do this as a means of self-protection, but it's usually counterproductive. When I used to have bad anxiety, I'd play out all the horrible scenarios that could possibly occur and create a game plan for each one so that I'd be prepared for the potentially traumatic outcomes of each. Even as a young kid in school, when I knew I'd have to read aloud in front of my class, I'd count how many students came before me so that I could prepare the section that I'd have to read when it was my turn! It's from this kind of fearful mindset, however, that thought energy can start interacting with matter to bring your negative assumptions to fruition—and nobody wants that. It's also possible to have positive feelings rooted in the future, but this typically doesn't happen until you've learned to more consistently sustain your high vibration. When you do, it feels like a knowingness that a situation will occur, and you're confident that all good things will happen.

The moment you become aware that you're living in the future in a positive way, your energy will start shifting for the better. You'll gain clarity, and it's with that lens that you will view your next steps. Manifesting is a lot like filling a container. If you relive bad programming or project a negative consciousness onto the future, a container that's already full of limiting thoughts, beliefs, and past traumas could lead to counter-manifestation—or at least, cause you to spin your wheels until you go mad! The good news is, you're learning all the tools you need to counterbalance this.

Question #5: What Do I Think Is Going to Happen?

Now that you've assessed your feelings, named what you suspect is causing them, and noted if they cause you to live in the past or future, it's time for a bold reality check. Just from asking yourself the prior four questions, you're already starting to transform your energy for the better. I tend to find that awareness is a huge part of your growth through this process. You've primed your mind for a change in thinking, though it will take a bit more work to arrive. Even so, ask yourself what you now think is going to happen, given what you feel and what you've learned about your feelings. You may still default to your usual assumption, but chances are, you'll do so with a little less doubt than before. This is normal but also progress.

Humans tend to approach the world with a sense of tunnel vision and finality that can take some effort to budge. We think *If I feel this way today, then I will feel this way forever*—instead of remembering that energy oscillates and what you experienced was just a moment in time and doesn't need to be your forever. My client Jan, for example, owns a nail salon, and for many years, found that every time she poured ad dollars into her business, she'd feel anxious when she saw the dent this left in her bank account. Though Jan knew that she had to spend money to make it—and that every time she made investments, she'd see a return on them—Jan grew up poor, and so her knee-jerk reaction was to feel momentarily convinced that the hole in her savings would last forever. This also illustrates our proclivity toward a negativity bias, which means we have a mentally hardwired tendency to register negative stimuli more readily and then dwell on these negative feelings and events. This can cause us to feel, for instance, the impact of reproach more powerfully than we feel happiness when we're praised. All these thoughts contribute to our vibration. It's so common to believe and think that what's happening now will last forever if it's bad, but when it's good, it won't last long at all. This is simply not true, and once you alter your programming, you'll be amazed that your mind could ever be so shortsighted!

Question #6: Is This Even Mine?

If you've noticed during a check-in that your feelings don't make sense or don't track back to past programming, there's a chance that what you're feeling is empathic energy coming from someone else or even multiple people at once. You know when a wave of energy hits you—whether it comes from your boss, a spouse, a friend, or a sensory experience like a smell or sound—because it changes how you feel. Again, these feelings impact you and your frequency, and whether they raise or lower it will affect your vibrational field to either become fluid or dense.

Because you exist in an energetic soup, you might find yourself absorbing energy that isn't technically coming from your own conscious or subconscious. And if you're not careful, you can grab hold of this and make it yours. Let's say that you wake up and feel anxious, but after asking yourself the prior five questions, you can't peg it to an experience that's triggering it.

Consider who you've interacted with in the past 48 hours. What friends or family members have you talked to, and what are they going through? How about the people who share your house, or especially, your bed (we release and share a lot of excess energy when we sleep)? Our remarkable ability to absorb others' energy reminds of me an actress that I worked with in Scandinavia, who wasn't seriously ill, but came to me to learn ways to optimize her physical health and mental peace. When we measured how much excess energy frequencies were coming from her body using our eductor device, her readings showed that she was carrying more energy in her field than what's normal or healthy. The reason, I soon discovered, was twofold: First, she was keeping a huge secret about her sexuality, which carried an abundant, negative frequency that showed up as anxiety, mental fog, and feeling generally "off." Second, this was compounded by the outside energy of her rabid fans who psychically attached their energy to hers, unknowingly and on a regular basis. This last part is what I believe tipped the woman's frequency over the edge. We helped her to rebalance her energy by first helping her feel safe about coming out to the public and reassuring her that her audience wouldn't stop loving her because of her sexual orientation (this meant detangling beliefs that she held about her own mother's love and their related thoughts). Once this weight was gone, her energy naturally elevated, which made it harder for others' energies to cling to her and make her feel badly.

If you suspect you've absorbed someone else's energy, you can easily clear it by doing one or more of the following clearing techniques: the simplest of these is taking an Epsom salt bath, exercising, doing a meditation, or spending time with those who naturally get you back into a high vibrational state. When you consistently exist at higher levels, the energy of others will become less likely to attach to you and instead flow through your field's filter and back into the universe.

What's Next?

As your check-ins progress, this practice will become instinctual, and you'll begin to check in with yourself any time you sense a positive or negative feeling that's affecting your vibration. Check-ins will also become integral to rewiring the brain. Though your brain constantly tweaks its own wiring, you are typically triggered by and focused on the same sore spots every day, and you react to them in similar ways. The reason your life may feel so cyclical is because you are constantly responding to stimuli according to the neurological pathways you have built in your brain over time. Electricity is sent throughout the brain as, say, you tell yourself the meaning of an event or interaction or a memory is revisited, and it tends to flow in a similar fashion to what it always has. But when you check in with yourself, you initiate neuroplasticity, which is where our brains rewire themselves, plus brain pruning, wherein new habits and thought patterns cause new neuropathways to be built. I see daily check-ins resulting in new neuropathways all the time.

My client Jean had a history of trauma, plus interpersonal conflicts due to religion, family issues, and a sudden divorce thanks to an unfaithful partner. She felt like a sad, lost cause and deemed herself "the worst manifester ever."

Jean and I began with small changes that made a big impact—daily check-ins were a must. She set an alarm on her phone three times a day for the first 15 days and wrote about how she was feeling each time that alarm went off. Jean did not like what she felt, and at first, it set her back. Shame, anger, and depression reared their ugly heads. "I am in even worse mental and emotional states than I thought," she initially recorded. "This is going to take years to fix. I have felt this way for as long as I can remember." Thankfully, Jean was wrong about her forecast. When she applied check-ins with the additional tools I'll share in coming chapters, Jean established a simple system that interrupted those states. This allowed her to begin painting on a fresh canvas.

Within a week, Jean said she felt "different." "Different" turned into "pretty good," and "pretty good" turned into "empowered" within three weeks' time! Six months later, Jean launched her own business and confronted family members with whom she had conflict. Today, she has a lovely boyfriend, and they travel the world together. Jean no longer needs my assistance in the same way as before, though she recently admitted that she still does check-ins when she's feeling off to bring herself back into a state of peace. "Otherwise," she told me, "I most dominantly feel gratitude and unconditional love throughout the day." And that's the goal!

Once you're a wiz at check-ins, let's move on to detangling your dense energy. This second proactive secret begins the process of working through your past programming so that you can manifest from a clean slate and prime your field to deliver the abundance you crave.

Tips and Takeaways

✦ Energetic check-ins teach you to become highly aware of the beliefs that inform your thoughts, which impact your vibration and ability to manifest.

✦ Though you will initially make an effort to check in, they'll soon become habit.

✦ Energetic frequencies are like waves that rise and drop all day, and when they do, our minds pour a ton of energy into their corresponding feelings. These feelings determine your dominant frequency, which sets the stage for manifesting conscious or unconscious desires.

✦ As you check in, the energy behind this practice should be one of cool curiosity and awareness.

✦ When negative energy strikes, it begins as an energetic imprint, then manifests in the emotional and physical body. Get ahead of, and heal, these feelings before they cause deeper problems.

✦ When you live in the past, you are either trying to re-create it or run from it.

✦ Because you exist in an energetic soup, you might absorb energy that isn't yours.

✦ The reason your life may feel so cyclical is because you are constantly responding to stimuli that trigger and retrigger the neurological pathways you have built in your brain over time.

More Resources and Free Downloads

If you enjoyed this chapter, I've put together a simple one-page "Energetic Cheat Sheet" pdf just for my book readers that reveals all my favorite ways to check-in, the exact questions I ask myself, and some sample situations on when it's an absolute must to do check-ins. Download it for free at www.authenticliving.com/gifts

Chapter 5

Secret #2

DETANGLE DENSE ENERGY

Imagine a fishing net that's all tangled up. Let's use this image to represent the unhelpful connections you have to your past, factors that negatively pull on you in the present, and all the different personas that you feel you have to take on in order to make yourself and others feel safe. Together, these factors create inauthentic versions of you that weigh your energy down.

There is always an original knot in your proverbial net that was formed the first time you created a disserving belief, and it's this belief that's led to upsetting thoughts and feelings, which over time, have become complicated with even more events and interactions that have reinforced and tightened the original tangle. The end result is a huge knot, or series of knots, that have created a dense, overwhelming, and confusing psyche, life experience, and energy field that feel virtually impossible to undo. Clearing your field is achievable, though, and to do this—plus raise your vibration and set the stage for seamless manifesting—you'll need to detangle the programming that's led to dense, blocked, and intertwined energy so that it frees you from the negative factors that thicken your field. Detangling gets you to the first knot that started the whole mess; then you can deal with its twists and turns and get yourself on a path to living your dream life.

In the last chapter, you learned how to check in with yourself, so your mind should be primed for some serious detangling. You learned to recognize how you feel at any given time and why you feel that way, if you're living in the past or future, what you expect the outcome of your feelings to be, and if what you're feeling is even yours or if you're empathically picking it up from someone else. In short, you became hyperaware of your feelings as a matter of course. So now that you're more connected to your emotions, which are tied to the thoughts that send out manifesting vibrations, it's time to investigate the roots of your negative programming and remove them. In this chapter, I'll teach you how to detangle your energy and inadvertently rewire your reactions and brain, so you can achieve and fully manifest your goals and desires.

Why Bother to Detangle Energy?

There are consequences to leaving dense, blocked, and tangled energy unchecked—and as you know, a decreased ability to manifest is high among them. By the end of this book, you'll have cleared your field and elevated your frequency so that you're manifesting from an optimal place; untangling the beliefs, thoughts, and feelings that contribute to dense energy will make this process a breeze. But why is this true, and how else will your life benefit from the practice?

Tangled, dense energy forces you to live in an inauthentic state that is not who you are at your core—that is, in your soul. This is not who God designed you to be, which is to say, not your highest self that thrives on high vibrational living. So if you don't deal with tangled, blocked, and dense energy, then you remain attached to the past and operating from a headspace that doesn't represent who you really are. This is very different from when you are your authentic self, and as a result, believe, think, and feel from a clean and elevated perspective and energy frequency. You essentially return to the purity you embodied as a baby. And the energy attached to this state is clear and has limitless potential to co-create with God. It's the form you were in before programming changed your identity and traumas skewed your self-perception. The big goal of detangling energy is returning to the person, and soul, you were divinely created to be.

If I think back to that pinnacle bathroom-mirror moment for me years ago, when I turned my life over to God and asked God to be used to my fullest potential according to a divine plan, I remember an energy washing over me that was loftier than anything I'd ever felt. I believe that what I experienced was the highest version of energy that my soul could reach in that moment and akin to the frequency I exuded before my life experience programmed me differently. It felt like pure, limitless potential. I've since channeled that we can all feel this energy, and it exists in a higher plane than even love energy, which I'd once thought to be the ultimate frequency. I like to call this frequency, which emanates from your most authentic self, "is" energy: It's the energy of all things, in complete unity, as one. It just is. Every time I strive for untangled energy, this is the finish line I envision.

If you don't deal with your dense energy, you will also continue to rehash the same negative situations and react the same way to low-vibrational stimuli and triggers that in turn, solidify certain patterns of behavior. This means you're not only operating from a low vibration that impedes manifestation, but you're reinforcing less than ideal neurological pathways. If you walk through a field in the same direction every day to get to your friend's house, a path starts to form, right? The grass begins to grow differently and after enough trips, if you were to tell someone to take the path you did, they'd see what you've already carved out. What's interesting is that each time you left home for that trek, your brain would involuntarily assume that this path is the easiest one that you can take. Your walk would become an automatic process, and you'd anticipate the trees, flowers, and grassy patches you'd see before seeing them. But just because this path is familiar, doesn't mean it's the simplest. There could be other ways of reaching your friend's house; you just haven't explored them yet, so you take what you perceive to be the path of least resistance, and in a very simplified way, your neurological pathways tend to act similarly.

Perhaps most important, untangling energy helps you to understand and navigate your relationships and circumstances with clarity, and since you're operating from a higher vibration, with more love too. Energetically, this lighter love frequency allows your mind to physiologically process information more lucidly. I'll talk more about the multifaceted power of love in Chapter 7, but it's worth noting here that embodying a love frequency was a game changer when I helped clients in Norway who suffered from psychosomatic illnesses due to various types of traumas. The frequency of love that I emitted in our sessions together allowed for their subconsciouses to "chill out," if you will, and kept patients from viewing change as a threat. This is important because when you feel lighter and think clearer, you'll begin to seek solutions that are of the highest good. What's more, this can encourage you to find ways to transform a situation or relationship for the better rather than eliminate it from your scope entirely. Once you reach a higher energetic state after detangling your field, you essentially turn the denseness of that old reality into a new and higher reality that's underscored with love.

I once had a client named Louise who had a painful relationship with her father, and the way that it impacted her was rooted in past programming. When Louise became his caretaker after he fell ill with dementia, the man became even more cruel and critical of his daughter. Right away, Louise felt that she had a choice to make to protect herself from her dad's attacks: she could play the dutiful daughter and allow it to destroy her, or she could hire a nurse and cut him out of her life completely. But once Louise's energy began to soften and raise after doing many check-ins and detangling energy, she realized that she had a third option: to be the solution to her problem. Her perspective began to clarify and shift. Louise began to see her father as a hurt child, in need of love, and began responding to him accordingly. As a result, he began to treat Louise more amicably too. Louise was able to transmute, rather than eliminate, the energy that supported her relationship with her father as they both became more loving versions of themselves. This was only made possible by the fact that she did the work to elevate her field.

Understanding Tangled Energy

As I mentioned, there are three major factors that create tangled energy: past programming, current challenges, and the personas that we create to help us and others feel safe. I'll explain how to do the detangling process later in the chapter, but for now, I'd like to illustrate just how easy and *normal* it is for your thoughts, feelings, and energy to become wound into metaphorical knots. I don't want you to feel, for one second, that having a low or dense energy field is something to feel ashamed of because this is the natural result of living on this planet and dealing with the challenges that come with it. During channeling sessions, I'm repeatedly told that we, as humans, are here to learn lessons and constantly grow from both our exciting and painful experiences. What's more productive to anticipate, instead, is how incredible you'll feel once you've gotten to the root of why you have the thoughts and emotions you do and how easy life will seem when you can flow through this 3D world with an air of ease and abundance. Doesn't that sound dreamy? You can even pause to imagine a light and burden-free feeling coursing through and around your body. I suspect this is close to what you'll sense with a high vibrational field. It feels amazing, right? Okay, now come back to me. You've got work to do!

As you might guess, past programming contributes to an enmeshed field because it's the complicated foundation upon which you've built your up-and-down life until now. It's fed, and continues to feed, your values and the rules that you live by. This would be terrific if your past were only full of encouraging messages and empowering memories, but of course, that's not even remotely realistic. Every one of us has imprints and traumas from our past programming that's twisted our beliefs and thoughts, even if they began with good intentions. My client Kristie was raised as a staunch Catholic, and as an adult, all she wanted was to manifest her perfect soul mate. Yet along with her religion's positive teachings, Kristie simultaneously learned that she was a sinner, which she internalized as meaning that she was an innately bad human. This created the thought that she'd surely sabotage any prospective good relationship that crossed her path. From there, her beliefs, thoughts, and feelings became even further validated and widespread over time, like when Kristie would lose touch with a friend or fight with her sister. Though she'd pray about these situations, they'd still fall apart, which only reinforced Kristie's suspicion that she was naturally bad and generated yet another skewed belief that if she asked for too much from God, God would tune her out and wouldn't provide. In no time, Kristie saw herself as a burden to everyone around her—and this caused her to doubt her ability to manifest a partner who'd love her unconditionally.

You can imagine how what began as a set of well-meaning values from Kristie's past programming grew and morphed into a tangled mess that ruined Kristie's self-image and reached across every facet of her life, plus kept her in a low vibration. From here, no matter how hard Kristie prayed or tried to move the manifesting needle, little went her way. It was only when she began to regularly check in with herself and then start to detangle the beliefs and thoughts that led her to her current mindset that she could remove the root problem that was creating inert energy and dampening her spirits. Until then, Kristie hadn't considered that her inability to meet a partner and fall madly in love was connected to a seemingly unrelated religious belief that she was taught as a little girl. Isn't it fascinating how our root beliefs can grow so many unwieldy branches in adulthood?

Negative factors in the present can also create dense, tangled energy. Recently, my friend Lala was telling me about an upsetting interaction she had with her cousin Barbara. Lala explained how Barbara felt so stressed because she owed money on back taxes— and rather than listen and sympathize with her, Lala found herself agitated and confused. She even wanted to lash out at Barbara for being so irresponsible! Before Lala let these feelings eat away at the connection between the two women, she checked in with herself and then went through the process of detangling her unusual reaction. Lala realized that certain factors in the now—she was dog-tired, on a deadline for work, and on edge from a loud and never-ending construction project at her house—were influencing how she responded to Barbara's story. Lala grasped, too, that these current factors had also become tangled with a childhood-based need to always feel compelled to solve other people's problems for them, and that money issues, particularly around tax season, were a threatening topic in her home growing up. You can see how current conditions became snarled with past emotions to create a convoluted reaction to Barbara's problem. Once Lala detangled the complicated snag, this elevated her energy, and she could support Barbara with the empathy she needed since Lala was now operating from her higher self.

I find that the most fascinating factor that contributes to tangled energy is the persona you take on to make yourself or others feel comfortable in any given situation. I developed my persona theory after working with multiple clients, as well as my own loved ones, who have dissociative identity disorder (DID), also known as multiple personality disorder, and realizing that every one of us creates personas to deal with problems and triggers (to be clear, I'm not saying that those with DID and the rest of us have the same experiences, just that these patients' experiences inspired a new and helpful way for me to excavate past programming). So, while you may not struggle with a DID diagnosis, every one of us does have personas that surface to fix our problems, protect us from certain feelings or repeat traumas, and help us or someone we know feel protected from harm. They stem from parts of our past that we've yet to reconcile.

Because of the check-ins, I'm sure it's now obvious that when you become aware of a feeling that needs to be addressed, the process is always initiated by a triggering event or interaction. Well, when you feel those feelings, your mind is responding from the perspective of your persona. For instance, when I was in my 20s, I dated a troubled man who cheated on me, plus called me fat all the time. He liked to pinch my stomach to insinuate that I had a lot of room for improvement. The moment he'd grab the skin on my belly, it would trigger a sense of self-loathing—and this became a persona for me. I believed I wasn't good enough for him, and soon felt inadequate in other areas too. I felt like a loser, and that became my persona when he and others triggered feelings of inferiority in me. Though it wasn't based in truth, this persona swooped in to handle/make sense of the situation for me—that is, my boyfriend finds me inferior, therefore I'm that person—and it did this from low, tangled energy. The energy was rooted in programming from my teens and 20s that insisted I was disposable if I didn't become someone that others wanted me to be. It turned me into an inauthentic people pleaser.

The thing is, you can't just disassociate from a persona. It's part of you and needs to be understood; a persona has a role to play, it is trying to be in control, and that underlying need will never go away. You can disarm your persona's beliefs, thoughts, and feelings, but I've found that it's very difficult to eliminate the driving needs of a persona since the memory it's attached to will always be part of you. Healing becomes a matter of working with and around a persona and its subsequent energy rather than eliminating it since you can never erase your past. So how do you meet your persona's needs but in an elevated way? Use it as the primo starting point for detangling the elements and energy that gave birth to the persona and low energy that sustain it.

Let the Detangling Begin!

Remember, when you check in with yourself after being triggered, you'll name your feelings, connect them to their cause, recognize if you're living in the past or present, consider what you think the outcome is going to be, and make sure that the energy you're feeling is even yours at all. Then you will start to detangle the energy—but only if you notice there are negative feelings and programming attached to your check-in. You do not need to detangle energy if you feel positive or happy because you are already in a rising vibrational state. And if you feel good, you'll have already considered how you got there and how to match and replicate that vibe during your check-in questions so that you can experience the feeling longer and more often. This practice is only for the single or repeat emotional reactions that hamper your day-to-day life.

Again, the easiest way to detangle programming and energy is to work with the persona you've created to deal with the trigger or problem at hand. So after you've checked in with your feelings, I'd like you to consider what persona your mind is using to understand or frame them. This will help you determine where your low state is coming from. Soon, you'll understand that what you feel right now isn't as amplified as you initially thought. It only feels like a major problem in the now because it's coming from unhealed thoughts based in the past or the future.

To help determine your persona, ask yourself three questions:

1. What am I telling myself right now?

2. What persona am I in, and what need does it have right now?

3. How can I meet this need in a more elevated way?

Let's say your brassy supervisor scolds you in a meeting, in front of your co-workers, for voicing an opinion that he does not share. You immediately feel anxious and want to either quit, hop a plane to Tahiti for a long vacation, or google a magic spell that will make you disappear forever. None of these are realistic options, however, so once you're back at your desk, you check in and run through your persona questions to figure out why you feel the way you do. You come to realize that you're telling yourself that you are afraid of losing your job and don't want to go bankrupt the way you did 10 years ago. Your persona, then, is Bankrupt You, and your need is to feel safe and provide for your family. Finally—and here's where your turning point begins—you realize that you can meet Bank-rupt You's need in a more elevated way by assuming a productive mindset. Why not update your résumé or take on a side job to boost your savings? Or if, in this now calmer state, you think you might be overreacting because your boss always seems to be in a bad mood lately, a walk around the block might be all that's needed. All these options ease your mind and make sense of your feelings, which positively change your energy.

Another trigger that I hear a lot, particularly from women, is a fear of rejection from fellow moms. Parents, and mothers espe-cially, put so much pressure on themselves to not only be perfect role models and providers for their children but also feel beloved and respected within their parenting peer groups. My client Cindy, for example, found herself triggered when she'd notice on Facebook that certain moms from her son's preschool class regularly met for coffee without inviting her. The first time this happened, Cindy plunged into self-loathing and felt abandoned. After checking in with those feelings, Cindy realized she was telling herself that the other moms rejected her because they could see who she really is—a person who's unlovable at her core. These feelings and the situation that caused them reminded her of when she was six years old and none of the other kids wanted to play with her on the play-ground. Cindy's persona, then, was Six-Year-Old Cindy, and the need of that persona was to feel included and good enough. Since she couldn't erase her memory or suddenly ingratiate herself with this mom clique, Cindy met her persona's need in a more elevated way by realizing that she didn't have to be part of this coffee klatch, and instead, could do a small act of self-care for herself to boost her mood (like a manicure or extra yoga class) and then call a few other friends, even though they weren't moms, to meet for coffee. This solution helped Cindy process her feelings and feel appreciated, which raised her vibe.

Like it did with Cindy, so many of our childhood experiences shape how we understand our adult lives. Studies show that children's personality traits have enduring effects that initiate and sustain certain life paths, not to mention your well-being in areas such as emotional and physical health, friendships, and mastery in chosen fields. And because your well-being as an adult is the result of a complex web of biological, social, and psychological influences that unfold over the course of your life, I believe that a persona that's rooted in childhood can have an extremely strong grip on your current reality. This was abundantly clear during an Authentic Living workshop, when a woman named Jen, who'd attended my conferences before, shared a powerful persona story with the group. She explained how a year prior, she and her husband were embroiled in an aggressive fight for full custody of her stepson since his biological mother wasn't psychologically able to provide a safe home for him. Leading up to their court date, Jen felt overwhelmed with an insatiable need to be heard and was at the point of tears, with the ardent belief that she'd have to fight harder than ever for her stepson because the world is unjust, the legal system is flawed, and life never goes her way. One night, when Jen was discussing the case with her husband, she began to sob really hard, yell through gritted teeth, and scream that nobody was listening to her about this life-changing decision. Jen's anger was so uncharacteristic and startling that her husband grabbed her by the shoulders and asked, "Who *are* you right now?" The question was a brash reality check for Jen, and she realized that in these heated moments, she wasn't her authentic self. Cue the check-in, persona work, and detangling . . .

Jen checked in and examined why she felt the way that she did about her stepson's complicated situation. She quickly realized she was telling herself that nobody respected or cared about the deep love and care she felt for the child—not because this was true, but because when Jen was 10 years old, her own parents got divorced, and she told the court that she wanted to live with her dad instead of her mom—yet the court did not grant this. The pivotal decision made for a bumpy childhood for Jen. Fighting for Jen's stepson now made her realize that she was in the persona of Ten-Year-Old Jen, who needed to be heard. But she realized that she could meet its needs in an elevated way, and without losing her mind, by asking her husband to give her a tight, tender hug anytime she spiraled out (this is a "pattern interrupt," which we'll discuss more in Chapter 6). The squeeze instantly calmed Jen down and brought her back to the present; her husband's love made her feel at peace, which raised her energy. If her husband were not around, she told me that she'd have hopped on her spin bike to work out the anger she felt and used the endorphin rush to override her negativity and help bring her back to center.

The more you run through check-ins and work through persona identities and detangling questions, the faster you'll become at these practices—again, because you'll be retraining your brain to quickly manage your emotions in these emotionally and energetically healthy ways. Eventually, when you become triggered by similar incidents, your brain's automatic default will be to prompt feelings of peace rather than anxiety and pain. It will understand that this is the easiest neurological pathway to take, and the simplest feelings to feel, because it is the path of least resistance. This will energetically transmit higher frequencies out into the universe on a regular basis, which is the sustained vibration needed to effortlessly manifest on a daily basis.

Making Sense of Leftover Beliefs and Thoughts

After detangling, you'll naturally find yourself in a more serene and reflective state. While the experience is still fresh in your mind, this is a great time for any lingering beliefs and thoughts that came to the surface of your conscious reel to further process and settle. To encourage this task, set aside time to go for a walk alone, sit quietly on your porch or under a tree, or journal in a tranquil spot. Your mind should feel quiet and relaxed, but if you feel triggered by revisiting the topics that set you off, skip this exercise. Otherwise, embrace your new perspective from a distance and consider this: What have you learned about your beliefs, thoughts, and personas so far?

Because all our personas come with a belief or set of beliefs that inform the thoughts and feelings that touch different parts of our lives, you'll start to notice which topics and themes regularly feature in your life. So if you're now aware that you feel rejected a lot, digest the beliefs and thoughts that swirled around these feelings. What still causes you to feel unworthy? What are you doing differently to help yourself? Are you able to move on without seeing these situations through a lens of permanency or negativity bias? Remember, our brains are always trying to create concrete realities to help us feel safe and sound, but that further determines the actions we choose in our environments and puts thought into deed, which is manifestation.

With some necessary psychological and energetic conditioning under your belt, you're now in a state of awareness and mental clarity. How will you sustain this? The next secret is to manage your triggers so that you can spend less and less time checking in and detangling.

Buckle up, it's a powerful one!

Tips and Takeaways

+ Three major factors create tangled energy: past programming, current challenges, and personas.

✦ Tangled energy forces you to live in an inauthentic state—not who God designed you to be.

✦ The goal of detangling energy is returning to the person, and soul, you were created to be.

✦ Pure, limitless potential exists on a higher plane than even love energy and emanates from your most authentic self. When you strive for untangled energy, envision this finish line.

✦ If you don't deal with dense energy, you rehash the same negative situations and react the same way to low-vibrational stimuli that solidify certain patterns of behavior. You operate from a low vibration that interrupts manifestation and reinforces negative neurological pathways.

✦ Everyone has imprints and traumas from past programming that's twisted their beliefs and thoughts, even if they began with good intentions.

✦ The more you do check-ins and work through persona identities and detangling questions, the faster you'll retrain your brain to quickly manage your emotions in energetically healthy ways.

More Resources and Free Downloads

If you enjoyed this chapter, I've put together a powerful daily meditation called "*Clearing and Releasing Dense and Negative Energy*" that will help you quickly release anything that is holding you back. I recommend you listen to it every night for 30 days to see some quick and lasting transformations . Download it for free at www.authenticliving .com/gifts

Chapter 6

Secret #3

MANAGE TRIGGERS
with
PATTERN INTERRUPTS

Learning how to manage triggers is at the heart of manifesting. And one of the simplest and most effective means to doing this is to master the use of pattern interrupts. These tools shift your emotions and redirect your energy when you sense a negative reaction to stimuli.

At this point, you're becoming a real pro at recognizing when you're triggered, understanding where your reactions stem from, and detangling the energy connected to their subsequent emotions. And the more you engage these practices, the faster and more intuitive this mental and energetic clearing process becomes. In all honesty, it really becomes as easy as pouring a cup of tea. But sometimes during your self-reflection, you might find that you need an energetic or emotional boost that you can't access from check-ins and detangling alone. Enter the pattern interrupt, which can be used as a floating tool at any point in time, whenever you need to quickly shift or reset your energy. This exercise is always available to you, so I hope it becomes a go-to tool that helps you to both maintain, and return to, a high vibration, as needed. The intention of a pattern interrupt is to immediately get yourself into a higher emotional state, and as you know by this point in our work, the higher your emotional state, the higher your vibrational state—as both directly impact manifestations and your overall quality of life.

As we delve into secret #3, I'll explain what pattern interrupts are, how and when to use them, why they have the power to destabilize triggers, and the role they play in helping to retrain the neurological pathways in your brain that are directly tied to your unconscious and eventually, more conscious manifesting abilities. I'll also discuss how pattern interrupts nudge you up an "emotional/vibrational ladder," which is basically a vibrational hierarchy of feelings. It's worth noting that I'd like you to use pattern interrupts in addition to check-ins and detangling, not in place of them. I mention this, because if you're anything like me, you'll fall in love with, and really lean on, your pattern interrupts for daily oomph! It's tempting to embrace the energy boost that they offer and just move on with your day, but pattern interrupts won't raise enough consistent energy on their own to improve your manifestation outcomes. Rather, they're a great way to create emotional distance from a triggered response or low vibrational state so you can get curious about why you're feeling the way you do. It's essential to do all the work that creates real change. No shortcuts here! But man, is it worth it to master the eight secrets. I promise!

We Now (Pattern) Interrupt This Program . . .

There are three types of pattern interrupts to keep on hand to access at any time and in any situation: physical, spiritual, and mental/emotional. It takes some trial and error to figure out which will help you and when since not every pattern interrupt will work for every person, trigger, or environment in which you're triggered. You may need a physical pattern interrupt after a spat with your spouse but a spiritual one when you're triggered at work—this is up to you. Because you and your past are so unique, it's impossible for me to tell you which exercises will work best at which times. I also like to leave room for your intuition to influence your choices here so you'll get increasingly used to trusting it while practicing the eight secrets. What's great is that once you find pattern interrupts that help, you'll have quick, all-access tools that offer instant, energetic gratification in the midst of various forms of chaos. I suggest finding at least three that work in each category so that you have options when you need them.

At their core, all pattern interrupts are meant to redirect your neurological wiring by way of physical, spiritual, and mental/emotional breaks in thought and energy. When you use a physical pattern interrupt, you use your body to distract or shift the emotional experience you're having in your mind. Doing 10 push-ups, a silly dance, singing a few lines from a favorite song, taking five deep breaths, or going for a brisk walk around the block are all physical pattern interrupts that my clients regularly tap. One of my favorite physical pattern interrupts, come winter at least, is snow rolling. When the ground is covered in mounds of white stuff, I like to run outside in a tank top and shorts and roll around in the snow for as long as I can tolerate. It resets my energy immediately! In warmer temps, I gravitate toward cold showers, which serve a similar purpose. They're known to increase endorphins, improve metabolism, boost circulation, and aid immunity. Now I'm going on record that they lift vibrations as well!

Spiritual interrupts either invoke a higher power or use your soul to shift your energetic frequency. Here, you might say a quick prayer, envision golden light streaming from the heavens and into your body, visualize angels assisting you in some way, or visualize rebalancing your chakras. Another great spiritual pattern interrupt is to mentally scan your body until you can sense where the energy feels densest. Do you feel tension in your shoulder, back, neck, or chest? Then, you'll picture a vacuum sucking away all that dark, tangled, and blocked energy and emptying it into the earth with love.

I once had a pair of clients named Kathy and Jim, who were married for 10 years but worried that their relationship was falling apart. After having kids, the two were butting heads more than usual, with Kathy defaulting to a controlling persona from her past programming and Jim, to a more childlike one from his. As a spiritual pattern interrupt, this duo decided they'd ground themselves by imagining roots, like those from a tree, growing from the bottoms of their feet and anchoring themselves in the ground. Their special twist, however, is that their mutual roots would intertwine with one another's to solidify their bond and divinely connect them. Imagining this calmed their thoughts and underscored their next steps with love.

Finally, a few mental/emotional pattern interrupts that engage the senses may be in order. I like listening to music, diffusing essential oils, and journaling. You could also borrow a pattern interrupt from my husband's arsenal: casting those who've upset you in a sped-up, Chaplin-esque, black-and-white movie to help minimize an otherwise heavy predicament by making it downright silly. If that doesn't resonate, it could be enough to reach out to a famously optimistic friend that you trust, a kind of accountability partner who will always help lift your mood. Remember, these are just some ideas that have worked for me and past clients, but feel free to be creative and come up with your own. No pattern interrupt is too ridiculous or strange when it aims to enhance your energetic, emotional, and mental states.

As you explore the best pattern interrupts that work for you, you may want to choose them based on whether you're primarily a visual, auditory, or kinesthetic learner. Since we're all wired differently, tapping into your basic instincts can yield speedy results. Visual learners, for instance, need to see pictures and graphs to visualize their way to solutions. Auditory learners prefer to hear information. Kinesthetic learners like to engage in an activity to grasp a concept. If you don't know which kind of learner you are, you can find a number of fun tests on the Internet to help. They're often based on the kinds of words you use, books you read, memories you store, and so on. Choosing a pattern interrupt that relates to your learning style is gently strategic since your brain will be more receptive to activities that naturally suit you and how you process data. I'm a very kinesthetic learner and find that pattern interrupts that involve movement make the biggest difference for me. One Christmas, a family member with whom I still have a sticky relationship called to catch up. Though he didn't say anything about our past, just hearing his voice triggered a flood of painful memories that made me feel like a vulnerable child again. When we hung up, I felt a heaviness that I couldn't shake. Before I could check in or detangle, I knew I had to use a pattern interrupt to stabilize myself. I took a few deep breaths, but that emotional weight was still there. I put my earbuds in, but my usual playlist couldn't shift my energy. Finally, I switched to salsa music and (almost aggressively) danced my heart out. I had to laugh every time I caught a glimpse of myself in the mirror, but moving my hips really did the trick. Engaging in an activity aligned with my learning style was exactly what my mind, emotions, and vibration needed. Once the song ended, I was able to quickly check in and detangle my response to the call, and it felt as if the conversation had never happened.

After you test out each pattern interrupt, ask yourself, *Do I feel different?* If you feel even incrementally better, add that practice to your collection. If you feel no change at all, think nothing of it and choose another. Know, too, that it can take using more than one pattern interrupt to feel a difference. You don't have to reach enlightenment or feel completely rectified after doing a pattern interrupt; you just have to feel better than where you were and have moved up the emotional/vibrational ladder, which I'll illustrate later in this chapter. Believe it or not, simply jumping from a feeling of shame to one of apathy, or from anger to neutrality, is a satisfying leap from your field's point of view. You can feel the relief when a pattern interrupt puts the breaks on an upcoming negative spiral. At its simplest, the clever exercise functions as a fun and forced, intentional pause that steadies you for whatever you reflect on, or do, next.

Warning: Triggers Ahead

As you know, a trigger is any stimuli that prompts you to recall an upsetting experience in a negative way, but let's look at triggers in the context of pattern interrupts. When you're triggered, the stimulus itself might seem benign to someone else, but *your* response is anything but. Nothing is a trigger unless your mind gives it that identity, either consciously or unconsciously. The trigger could be a smell, sound, conversation, place, voice, memory, name, or simply looking in the mirror and not liking what you see. Your brain churns: you're never going to be happy, lose weight, make more money, feel safe . . . and this loop weighs down your field and must be stopped and redirected, which is where the pattern interrupt comes in.

Triggers are so powerful, because they're a big part of the stories we tell ourselves about the world we live in. Triggers stem from past programming, and influence our beliefs, thoughts, and feelings. So much of our physiology is built for self-protection, and if our brains are involved in keeping us safe, the best way they can do that is through memory recollection. If you burn your hand on a stove, your mind will associate stoves with heat. You'll always think, *If this stove was hot before, it is going to be hot again*—regardless of whether the stove is even turned on. Unless you've cleared the trauma that's related to the stove being hot, you'll react as if it is hot every time you go near it. That being said, I try not to think of triggers as "bad," a sign that you're unhealed, or as a manifestation block. In an ideal world, we'd all take an objective step back and reframe our triggers as juicy feedback. When you feel triggered, what are you telling yourself when it happens? Triggers show up so that you can resolve their core beliefs and go on to manifest a happy life. They're messages that tell us what's ready to be understood and transmuted.

A common example of how we use a trigger to help us feel safe—when in actuality, it does the opposite—is how so many of us self-sabotage romantic relationships. After leaving an abusive marriage, my friend Brenda had a hard time finding a stable partnership, but she didn't know why. As an outsider, however, it was obvious to me that she kept re-creating familiar, dysfunctional scenarios in her new relationships so that she'd feel comfortable. For instance, immediately after Brenda was intimate with a man for the first time, she'd shut down. Intimacy was a trigger for Brenda, because in her marriage, this was the only way that she felt connected to and loved by her ex—even when he'd ignore her afterward. To protect herself from future apathy, Brenda would often push her new partners away first—in theory, before they'd have a chance to do this to her—and inadvertently cause them to break up with her. Sex was an unrelenting trigger for Brenda, and she wasn't able to meet a long-term partner until she acknowledged her trigger and detangled her programming. When she finally met the man she'd eventually marry, she was well on her way to healing, and any time she felt unsafe after sex, she'd clap her hands three times before checking in and detangling. Soon, Brenda was able to have an open, vulnerable, and honest relationship with her new man, and they are still together.

Until you've sufficiently worked through your traumas and programming, triggers can feel like harrowing reminders of your past that are unpredictable, massive, and able to cause you to overreact mentally (with untrue beliefs and thoughts), emotionally (by, say, crying or feeling scared), or physically (think vomiting or shaking). And if left to run rampant, all of these responses have energetic repercussions. But when you invoke a pattern interrupt, you throw up a wall in your mind that keeps your psyche from falling back fully on its automatic, negative, emotional reaction. You also stop related frequencies that are attached to this response from firing so you can process and reframe the situation using energy that's for your highest good. Neuroscience shows that your brain can increasingly welcome the frequencies associated with pattern interrupts as the new normal. The next time you use one, your state will elevate a little more than the last time you benefited from it. Eventually, you'll become completely desensitized from the trigger, so your energy can then be used to help you live in a healthier and happier way.

Triggers, Big and Small

While we're talking triggers as they relate to pattern interrupts, it's worth mentioning that I like to divide triggers from past programming into two categories: macro and micro. A macro trigger is a trigger that is obvious and upsetting. Here, you experience a sound, smell, taste, or event that throws you for a loop—maybe your mom yells at you or you get a whiff of a familiar cologne—and as soon as it happens, you feel an immediate shift to a lower emotion than what you originally felt. A micro trigger, on the other hand, sneaks up on you. Say, you catch your partner looking at your bum with a weird face, and then five hours later, you find yourself wondering if you should do a set of squats or treat yourself to new jeans because you suddenly feel self-conscious about how you look. A micro trigger still shifts you emotionally, but you don't recognize the inception point right away. It takes self-reflective sleuthing to figure out.

Through check-ins, you'll become increasingly aware of your macro and micro triggers, but you only need to do a pattern interrupt when you experience macros. They're the easiest to recognize in your field on a daily basis since micro triggers are more subtle and chronic. Eventually, you'll be able to notice and address micro triggers, but for now, it's enough to become aware of your most apparent triggers so that you can get in the habit of elevating those.

All this talk of macro triggers and pattern interrupts makes me think of the time my husband and I were having a heavy conversation about sourcing funds for an investment. Typically, we enter into new ventures with excitement, but we'd been hitting logistical walls on this project and our discussion began to feel unsettling the longer it went on. Finances can be a daunting macro trigger for me due to my own past and programming, and watching me get upset is a macro trigger of my husband's since his upbringing makes him uneasy around conflict. So when I found myself getting frustrated about our situation, and I noticed my husband shifting in his seat, I knew we had to do a pattern interrupt. We did a quick check-in and detangling session, which only took a few minutes because we've been using the eight secrets for so long that this process has become second nature to how we communicate. When we were done, we decided that our pattern interrupt would be to simply switch our conversation to an area of growth about our company that was seemingly unrelated but very exciting and high vibe. About 25 minutes into this, I got an e-mail from a donor offering a large sum of money—larger, in fact, than what we'd hoped for! By focusing on a higher vibrational conversation and releasing the potentially heavy and downward spiral we could have taken, my husband and I interrupted the negative flow and redirected our emotional, energetic, and mental states to lighter and more empowering ones. We manifested a practical and profitable outcome that was better than we'd expected!

When to Use Pattern Interrupts

As I'm sure you've noticed, pattern interrupts can be used any time you feel triggered. Perhaps the initial trigger is so startling that to get your hands to stop shaking and your mind to even focus on a check-in, you have to stop and do 10 jumping jacks first. If a trigger gets you down, you'll find it hard to solve a problem with the same mentality that got you there in the first place. My client MaryAnn, for instance, was newly divorced when her car broke down on the side of the road. For her, this was more than an accident; it was a triggering event that reminded her of how many problems she now had to handle without her spouse. Instead of trying to check in through a tsunami of tears, she paused to sing "I'm a Yankee Doodle Dandy" first! It was so silly that it made her smile, calmed her down, and mentally and energetically positioned her to continue with the check-in and detangling processes while waiting for AAA to help her out. She used a pattern interrupt to help her find a moment of clarity and the ability to change her state so that her energy was poured into healing and addressing her problem from an elevated frequency.

Pattern interrupts come in handy once you start clearing your energy too. You might find that the questions you ask yourself during the check-in and persona work of detangling brings up thorny memories and feelings, no matter how curiously detached you try to be, so pausing to use a quick pattern interrupt to diffuse those emotions helps. My friend Genny once told me a story about how, growing up, her mom used to shame her for gaining weight. This left an indelible impression on her, and as an adult, Genny worked really hard to embrace her natural curves despite her mom's insults. One summer, Genny went on a girl's trip with her friends to Florida. When it came time to hit the beach, Genny opted to keep her cover-up on as her bikini-clad friends urged her to take it off and have a good time. They had loving intentions, but the more Genny's friends prodded her, the more upset she became. Genny decided to grab drinks for the group as an excuse to escape their attention, and on her way to the bar, began to reflect on why she wanted to disappear so badly. Halfway through Genny's check-in, she saw she was living in the past and became even more upset. She felt angry at her mom *and* friends and couldn't tell the difference between them. Confused and overwhelmed, Genny used a pattern interrupt: She closed her eyes, took five deep breaths, and tilted her face toward the sun. The warmth, sea breeze, and fresh air grounded Genny enough to finish her practice and return to the girls. She wasn't ready to take off her cover-up, but she was able to enjoy the rest of her trip with a fresh perspective.

You can also end the check-in and detangling process with a pattern interrupt as a grand finale that gives your energy a well-deserved boost. This is best when you want to go really deep to understand a persona first by allowing it to play out without breaking the energy that's causing your pain. When a client named Kim attended one of my events, she felt enormously triggered that others in the group were getting the recognition she craved. I noticed she was acting out—hanging off the edge of a sofa, making snide comments under her breath—but I let this go so both she and I could gather more information about the persona from which she was behaving. After some time, Kim raised her hand and whined, "When are you going to help *me*?" At this point, I had enough "proof" that Kim was acting out an attention-seeking persona from childhood, so it made sense to finish her check-in and detangling session with a pattern interrupt. We landed on a guided meditation that let Kim drop into her heart space and feel seen. Even better, she took this practice home with her to use when she felt triggered, and in no time, Kim happily reported that her needy persona acted out less and less over the coming months.

A final option is to use a pattern interrupt as a stand-alone practice when your trigger is small or familiar, and either there's not a lot of work to be done around the subject or you don't have time to do a full check-in and detangling session when you're provoked. If a conversation about your roommate's sloppiness is a topic that triggers you a few days a week, you probably don't need to check in and detangle this every time he leaves his socks on the living room floor. In this case, it's enough to go for a quick run—or even grab your own socks and make a sock puppet show to make yourself laugh—and work out any frustrated feelings you have. A stand-alone pattern interrupt might also be useful if you need to calm your frantic nerves before heading into a pitch meeting at work—a quick prayer to your guardian angel could help. Here, the trigger is stressful, but your response is mild enough to put off a check-in until after the meeting.

It Is All in Your Head

While emotions aren't easily measured, your natural default to triggers happens in the brain's limbic system, which controls your fight-flight-freeze response and seems to occur almost instantly. Yet because the limbic system is part of your brain, you have the ability to alter how it interacts with pattern interrupts. So instead of having an automatic negative response to a trigger that comes from your past programming, the pattern interrupt teaches the brain to instead experience a trigger to **welcome** a pattern interrupt and then make a conscious choice as its preferred response. The pattern interrupt serves as a moment for the brain to take a deep breath before it defaults to fight-flight-freeze mode. It also doesn't allow the neurological pathway that's already been created, and is consistently activated by stimuli, to receive the same electrical charge that has so far influenced your beliefs, thoughts, and feelings. Remember, this is why we have seemingly "automatic" responses to most triggers; the negative pathway is prebuilt. But because pattern interrupts diffuse emotions and change your energy, your trauma's and past programming's grip loosens, causing new and improved pathways to replace old negative ones.

Using a pattern interrupt is a powerful choice that puts you in charge of your future. You are not a victim of your past or any of its consequent feelings. In fact, neuroscientists have discovered that the physiological life span of an emotion in the body and brain is only about 90 seconds. That's it! Ninety seconds! A sensation will arise, peak, and dissipate on its own. And then after that 90-second period, you *choose* to hang on to that emotion, whether it's a subconscious decision or not. Either way, every time you cue that emotion or reaction, you recycle, reinforce, and amplify it. The emotion's pathway refires. Your brain runs the manifesting show, but when you view it as an organ that can be reprogrammed with pattern interrupts, you're the one who's in control.

Movin' On Up!

Your energetic field responds to different emotions at different rates. So, when you're using the eight secrets to lay a foundation for effortless manifestation, one of the things you're doing is striving for higher emotions that give off higher vibrations that the universe can match with goals in your highest good. Earlier in the chapter, I mentioned that one of the aims of a pattern interrupt is to bump you up on the emotional/vibrational ladder. By climbing this hierarchy, even a little bit, you're elevating your emotional and vibrational state to ease with manifestation.

Here is that progression of emotions, listed from the highest to lowest frequencies they emit. I suggest copying this onto a piece of paper and posting it above your computer or on your refrigerator for easy reference. This way, you can turn to it whenever you want to match your feelings to their relative frequencies and understand them within the context of other emotions.

Highest

ENLIGHTENMENT
PEACE
JOY
LOVE
CLARITY
ACCEPTANCE
POTENTIAL
NEUTRALITY
COURAGE
EGO
ANGER
LONGING
FEAR
GRIEF
APATHY

Lowest   SHAME

So how does the emotional/vibrational ladder work in the context of manifesting? To keep things simple, all you need to know is that higher emotions like love, peace, and joy have higher vibrational fields, whereas fear, shame, and anger vibrate at a very slow rate. The goal of a highly effective manifester is to move the energetic particles in their fields at a faster rate by moving up the emotional/vibrational ladder, which travels from lower and more dense emotions to higher and lighter emotions. The reason for making sure you are always moving up this ladder is so you can move particles at a quicker pace and manifest in a faster and more positive way.

To put it another way, moving up the ladder allows you to manipulate matter faster and easier, and always to your betterment and in the highest good of all concerned. The inverse means that when you don't interrupt an energetic wave that creates a dense field, it can sabotage you for weeks or even months. Everything around you will react to your lower field too. It's true that you can smile all day to force a "fake it 'til you make it" happiness, which could improve your rapport with others, but a genuine emotion must be coming out of you to effectively raise your vibration. The truth is when the brain believes that something is a lie, manifestation doesn't work. Plain and simple. Your spirit, beliefs, and mind all have to be on board or else your conscience will not believe that it's possible to manifest that reality. It can become so overwhelmingly discouraged that it shuts down your ability to create anything at all. However, if there is a part of you that feels a goal *can* happen, even slightly, then it inches up your vibration to make it so. The easiest way to do this is to get yourself to the emotional state that you hope the goal might create. You want to jump up the vibrational scale so that you no longer see a situation as emotionally impossible to achieve; the brain will work with you rather than against you.

Now that you're better able to manage and manipulate triggers, I think a little self-love is in order. It's important to infuse everything that you do with real love, and self-love especially, because it helps you to remember that you're part of a much greater and unconditionally loving whole. When you can see that it softens your vibration, and opens you up to a higher acceptance of all things—including yourself. It's from this frequency that awesome manifestations occur.

Tips and Takeaways

✦ There are three types of pattern interrupts: physical, spiritual, and mental/emotional.

✦ With a physical pattern interrupt, your body shifts your mind's emotional experience.

✦ Spiritual interrupts either invoke a higher power or use your soul to shift your frequency.

✦ Mental/emotional pattern interrupts engage one or more of your senses.

✦ Triggers are powerful because they're part of the stories we tell ourselves about the world we live in. Triggers stem from programming and influence our beliefs, thoughts, and feelings.

✦ Use pattern interrupts to diffuse thorny feelings that come up during check-in and persona work.

✦ Pattern interrupts teach the brain to take a deep breath before it defaults to fight-flight-freeze.

✦ Pattern interrupts bump you up on the emotional/vibrational ladder to ease manifestation.

✦ Love, peace, and joy have high vibrational fields; fear, shame, and anger vibrate slower.

✦ Moving up the ladder lets you manipulate matter faster, easier, and always to your betterment.

More Resources and Free Downloads

If you enjoyed this chapter, I've put together a downloadable pdf called "*The Ultimate Guide to Pattern Interrupts: Visual, Auditory, and Kinesthetic*" that reveals my favorite types of pattern interrupts to use when I get triggered. Download it for free at www. authenticliving.com/gifts

Chapter 7

Secret #4
SEEK SELF-LOVE

Back in 2016, when I was researching and testing the efficacy of my therapy and coaching techniques in clinical settings, I became known for my ability to create an environment for clients that allowed them to cut down, by large percentages, the amount of time that they needed to heal the psychosomatic root causes of their health conditions. While my practices and methodologies were solid, I believe that a huge contributor to my success was much less tangible than what the intellects around me suspected. I believe the key to so much healing was *love*. And seeking self-love is the next secret we'll uncover.

While in the medical facility, I remember discussing my techniques with a wonderful psychiatric nurse who shadowed me so that she could learn my methodology. I ran through the practical measures that I took to help patients—and then I let her in on how to infuse it all with love. I explained that before working with a client, I'd get myself into an energetic state that was grounded in both intuition and affection. I'd create an energy within my-self that allowed me to profoundly and unconditionally love the person who needed me, plus exude the feeling that I knew they'd get better—and I did this by treating them as if they were *already* whole and well. I was never taught to act or think this way; rather, I instinctively knew it was essential to a patient's healing. After a great deal of discussion, the scientists and doctors that I worked with concluded that using heartfelt communication techniques helped patients let down their guards when they experienced trau-matic triggers and thought patterns at the root of patients' physical illnesses. This made them more willing and able to work through their past and, therefore, heal faster. I also believe that the patient's subconscious, which is built for protection, didn't feel threatened when they felt genuine love all around them. Love's high vibrational energy made our clients feel safe and eager to create this powerful frequency and emotion within themselves.

I realize it might sound hokey and perhaps even unrealistic to credit something as ephemeral as feeling love in a clinical setting to a person's long-term improvement outside a hospital. But again, the type of love that I'm referring to is a high-frequency emotion and highly memorable feeling, and when you feel unconditionally accepted and cared for, with no goal in mind but wellness, your de-sire to protect yourself from traumatic triggers and personas breaks down. When I viewed these patients as perfectly created and with deep approval of all that they were, the positive energy that they felt was both thick in the air and full of a love that they claimed to have never experienced. And when they felt this unconditional accep-tance, they could turn it inward, love themselves, and finally view themselves as perfect beings under God. Self-love is always our pie-in-the-sky emotion since there's a limit to how much love we can feel from outside sources. When you sincerely believe you're a perfect human creation who's worthy of your desires, you can break through so many of the psyche's fallacies and programming that's been reinforced over time. You feel a clear and pure truth once again through that connection.

A lesson in self-love follows the check-in, detangling, and pattern interrupt work you've done because at this point, you're emotionally and energetically ready to experience and recognize this very high vibration. It's not a sensation that you can fake, and for this frequency to resonate with the universe, your emotions must be authentic. You've also done a lot of mental work so far, and learning self-love makes for a nice breather between practices. What a great reminder that the manifestation process can be fun and feel great too! I always say, my work has expanded to the extent that it has today because it's fun and rewarding; adding as much love to the process as possible only amplifies the magic of rapid manifestation. Soon, love will become your natural way of being. What began as a proactive goal will just become your reality.

In this chapter I will explain how practicing self-love and surrounding yourself with unconditional love will raise your vibration, offer a supreme frequency that attracts your desires, calm neurological pathways, transform how you frame your past, and bring you back to a state of centeredness and connectedness that allows life to fall gently into place. And since unconditional love sits close to the frequency of enlightenment on the emotional/vibrational ladder, when you're able to turn this emotion inward, manifestation becomes so much easier. For years now I've been channeling that the next step for humanity is to embody unconditional love, which will help elevate the collective consciousness on our planet. This will also help bring about your greatest wishes and align you with the universe's delivery of the highest good for all concerned.

All You Need Is Self-Love

I've come to learn that those who either refuse, or simply don't feel, love will demonstrate behaviors that stem from scarcity, in-authenticity, and loss. They may focus on self-protection or even people-pleasing, rather than operate from their highest self and their cleanest energetic and emotional slates, because their thoughts and actions don't stem from faith. Believing in the possibility of change is at the heart of every manifestation effort. So I've realized that if I can lovingly help you see your worth, perfection, and purpose—in other words, help you feel accepted and adored, which is the op-posite of feeling scarcity and loss—then your empowered beliefs and related, higher frequencies will embed themselves in your mind and energy field. You'll feel this new truth that strongly, and it will resonate with who you are, deep in your soul.

Now no matter how much I remind you that you're a perfect and beloved human, the reality is that you might not feel my en-ergy from the words on this page in the same way that, say, my Norway patients did or an event attendee does in person. Before writing this book, I did ask God to help you feel my love as you read, but I hope you will assume the task of absorbing what I'm saying, turn this love inward, and feel it for yourself. Because when it comes to manifesting, I've come to believe that self-love is the engine that fuels limitless potential in so many ways. It puts you on a high vibration where limitless creation is possible, and it psycho-logically allows you to both dream about what you want and accept the possibility that anything can happen because you believe that you're worthy of receiving it. Pause for a moment and ask yourself: if you could do anything, and lacked nothing, what would you want and do for yourself and others? This is the question that self-loving manifesters pursue every day.

On the other hand, when you feel robbed of love, you live in a state of basic survival with all your priorities built around avoiding pain rather than running enthusiastically toward love. When our lives don't look the way we'd like, we take love away from ourselves—despite the fact that love is one of the most powerful frequencies that let us create what we want. But if your world isn't as you imagined, you might typically feel shame, regret, and/or disgust and begin to see yourself as fundamentally flawed and unworthy. You experience vibrational contradictions of love that originate with fear, loss, inadequacy, and lack. Now to fix this, you can't just pour love into an old trauma or wound; you have to dig it out from under the rubble of your programming so that you process and manifest from a clean and loving state. Your shovel, so to speak, is of course the collective eight secrets that you're learning in this book—particularly the check-in and detangling processes. From here, your heart opens up to the idea of self-love and encourages you to make choices from the high vibration that comes from clearing your past and starting fresh from an open and beautifully vulnerable point of view.

I'll never forget a client I'll call Brian, who attended one of my Authentic Immersion events over the course of 10 days. Right away, I had a hunch that he'd experienced sexual trauma in some way (I have a sixth sense for sniffing this out). On the outside, Brian really held it together: he had a beautiful family, was in terrific health, had an upbeat attitude—the works. But I instinctually felt that he was suffering on the inside. Toward the end of the retreat, Brian shared that when he was a preteen, he molested his neighbor. He did this once, and it ruined his entire emotional life until he came to my event. You can imagine the guilt and shame Brian felt—not to mention, the tremendous self-loathing that infiltrated his programming. He felt unworthy of a good life and saw himself as a monster. Though Brian thought he'd been doing all the right stuff to love away his pain—eating well, staying fit, getting rest, spending time with his family—none of it healed him because his self-improvement tactics stemmed from fear and secrecy, and not true self-love. Brian had tried to mold himself into his "best self," not because he wanted to nurture who he was and spread that love to others but because he hoped to compensate for the awful person that he feared he was.

For Brian, it took a lot of checking-in, detangling, persona, and pattern interrupt work for him to receive and internalize his family's and community's love, which eventually led to him forgiving himself for what he'd done 50 years prior. First, however, he had to deeply accept that while he made a grievous mistake, a greater, unconditional love existed for him that wasn't based on actions or inactions. Once Brian believed that this could come from both him and God, without a doubt in his mind, he was able to practice and actually feel acts of forgiveness. He began to believe his wife when she said she loved him, looked at himself in the mirror without horror, treated himself well because he felt he deserved it rather than to compensate for angst—and experienced the higher vibration that came with welcoming self-love in its most accessible and genuine forms.

When I channel the relationship between past programming and our ability to embrace self-love, I'm shown that traumas create a kind of emotional and energetic fractioning off of who we are, but self-love can make us whole again. Remember, if a deep enough trauma happens or you experience a profound enough low frequency, even over time, your psyche can split off to help compartmentalize related feelings; from there, if you don't deal with them, you create a persona with its own set of fearful beliefs that influence your thoughts and feelings. You revert back to what you've been psychologically programmed to feel and do rather than operate from an elevated state. The obvious problem with fear-based any-thing is that it is so dense that it makes the energy around you slow down. And while fear is a useful response when you see a tiger darting toward you, because it motivates you to save yourself, this primal reaction gets in the way when you tap into it every time you're startled—especially when you're working on manifestation skills. What's healthier and more effective at understanding your response for long-term healing is to translate a fearful feeling into one of curiosity. Ask yourself, *Why am I feeling so afraid right now?* You don't want to run from fear but transmute it. And if you can use the powerful energy of self-love to encourage and underscore this process—questioning your fear with curiosity, because you value your long-term energetic and mental health—this fresh headspace can reinforce the new and more positive neurological pathways that you're building.

When it comes to healing negative vibrations with self-love, I'll never forget a tight embrace that I received from a woman named Amma, a "Hindu hugging saint," when I was in my 20s. As I lin-gered in that woman's strong arms, and she chanted in my ear, I felt as if all my broken pieces were gluing themselves back together because Amma oozed unconditional love; it was her magical salve. And because Amma's love felt so good, every bit of me soaked it in; its warmth and safety reminded me of how I imagine I felt as an incoming soul to this world, before life wore me down, buried this love, and made it inaccessible for far too long. When Amma let go, I realized that in contrast to her pure love, what I'd been giving to others all these years wasn't love but self-sacrifice, people-pleasing, and complicated, emotional reactions to unrelenting manipulation. So I began to make self-care and self-love a priority to counteract this programming and teach myself what it is to feel and give true, potent love—and the process felt like being reborn. When you feel new and whole again, your energy becomes pure potential, similar to what you possessed when you first came into existence. You have no programming, worries, or lower vibrational feelings, thoughts, and beliefs. You only give off and feel love around and within you, and even if it's hard to believe when things get tough, this state is most natural to us and the one from which the best conscious and unconscious manifesting occurs.

Practicing Self-Love

At first, practicing self-love may need to be a deliberate effort. Especially if you have a daunting past, it may not intuitively flow in and around you. Nonetheless, I believe that self-love is as essential to human existence as breathing and drinking clean water, so at first, you'll want to make a concerted effort to provide care and compassion for yourself. Over time, you won't have to chase self-love every day since you'll innately feel it and know that it's everywhere. Your perception becomes clearer once you've detangled a past that was blinding you to love and self-love. It also really helps to put faith in a higher power because God is the ultimate source of unconditional love. I believe God is in all things and everywhere, which means that no matter how my material world lets me down, I'm still surrounded by God's love and worthy of it at all times. If you know there's nothing you can do or not do, and still feel love, then you don't have to revolve your life around receiving, connecting, or pursuing love in unhealthy ways.

Love is there for the taking.

Nourishing self-love is not about giving yourself regular bubble baths and pedicures and then returning to your usual self-flagellation. At its deepest level, self-love involves trusting yourself, feeling connected to who you are and what you believe, and asserting boundaries when you encounter fear-based beliefs; these values can better connect you with others too. Self-love also means prioritizing peace and speaking lovingly, or at least more gently, to yourself when you're down. Studies have linked self-love to increased resilience and an ability to see things from a new perspective. Whenever my clients feel unconditional self-love, they tell me that they feel calm, centered, grateful, and happy. They also feel inspired to manifest and realize that they're in a state that allows them to feel, experience, and become a person they weren't able to access in denser mindsets. When you don't practice self-love, those same studies show that you feel more stress, anxiety, and reactivity to little irritations that you might have otherwise ignored. Daily life feels like more of a struggle, tasks feel more overwhelming, and the emotional void can lead to feeling drained and miserable. You may feel a general emptiness or resentfulness toward others or yourself as well. When you are experiencing high vibrational and authentic love on a daily basis, however, you become more present for the events and people you care about, including yourself.

One of the greatest acts of self-love I've learned to give myself is permission to establish boundaries. I used to be overly accommodating, regardless of how healthy or morally just I thought my efforts were. For instance, I'd work 14-hour days even when I was ill, try to nourish relationships with men who cheated on me, and financially support anyone who needed my help, even if they didn't earn or deserve it. I even stayed friends with a man who'd abused me for a while! It wasn't until my husband pointed out that I often tethered myself to unhealthy bonds from the past that I realized 1) my people-pleasing was a trauma response to avoid conflict and 2) it reflected how little self-love I had. I began blocking numbers, having hard but truly loving conversations with aggressive family and friends, and ending relationships with those who hurt me past what should have been the point of no return. These boundaries were so freeing to establish and experience that I lovingly swung my pendulum in the opposite direction, and today, I'm shockingly transparent in all my relationships—personal, romantic, business, and otherwise. It is a huge relief and leaves room for me to give more of myself to those who deserve it. At times, such boundaries also create a space for others to recognize and heal their own personas, triggers, and unhealthy behaviors—rather than have me support and reinforce them.

Countless factors get in the way of feeling unconditional love for yourself, but don't give them another thought because there should be nothing that you need to do, be, or experience to feel love. Playing comparison games among friends and family—like keeping up with the Joneses' house, car, or seemingly perfect family—will chip away at the expansive vibration of self-love because it invalidates your true essence. A lack of self-love also keeps you from honoring your values and living in a way that aligns with them. Showing up in the world as someone who speaks and lives their truth is a remarkable sign of self-love, and it encourages others to do the same. The alternative is to get hung up on your flaws or the ridiculous errors made in front of those whose opinions you care too much about. Here, you fall into self-criticism, shame, and insecurity—which generate low vibrational energy. You must trust and forgive yourself when times are hard, and always stand by what you believe in.

If you have trouble getting yourself into a self-love mentality, think about treating yourself with the generosity, affection, and kindness that you would a loved one or child. Here, you might speak more gently to yourself, and with more respect. Positive self-talk that stems from self-love will pull you through a tough experience more easily. Your nasty inner voice will likely disappear and be replaced with one that is kind and respects who you are. It will forgive your mistakes and refuse to see your perceived shortcomings in an abusive way. You'll no longer settle for less than you deserve because you'll appreciate your value and that of all other beings too.

I've found that self-love can keep depression and anxiety at bay as well because it helps you either forgive yourself when life events go sideways and release the noose of self-judgment—or see upsetting situations from a more uplifting perspective. My client Bella had what she felt was a horrible past: her brother passed from an overdose, her mother died at a young age, she left an abusive marriage, and her son suffered from trauma due to that marriage. These cumulative insults made it hard for Bella to get out of bed in the morning; her depression and anxiety were too much to bear. It didn't take long to work through Bella's programming once she was ready to infuse her days with self-love. She did this by specifically targeting the roots of her depression and anxiety. Bella realized her depression was mostly caused by the guilt she felt for her son's trauma and from financial issues caused by her divorce. Bella's self-love activities, then, aimed to counteract these: she planned quality-time activities with her son that demonstrated her love and made Bella feel good about initiating them, and when she felt triggered while balancing her checkbook, she'd remind herself that her higher power loves her supremely and would always take care of her. Bella also realized that if she could create more love in her life, she'd be able to gift it to her son, and while she couldn't change his traumatic past, she could positively impact his future this way. Her heartfelt plans and reminders were simple acts of self-love, but not to be underestimated. She's since become a successful life coach, and her son's become a mentor to kids who are bullied in school. By encouraging her son's self-love, he now extends it to others.

All that being said, what I don't encourage is selfishness disguised as self-love. These priorities are so often confused, especially because we're in a sociological moment when putting your needs first and saving yourself at all costs are considered acceptable routes to happiness. How many times have you heard someone say that you should do whatever you want, so long as it makes you feel happy, comfortable, and untroubled as a result? The dilemma here is that any pursuit of joy that does not come from pursuing the highest good of *all* carries a low frequency. One of my favorite quotes from author L. R. Knost is this: "Taking care of yourself doesn't mean 'me first.' It means 'me, too.'" And I feel that's so true and especially applicable here. The ego can be sneaky, so always lead with your heart and intuition when making satisfaction fueled choices of any kind. Selfish actions that you decide to call self-fulfillment are not honored as self-love. Self-love involves setting admirable standards that respect your needs *and* the needs of those around you. When you love yourself, you will have more compassion for others and see the genuine transference that takes place versus calling something love that is not love at all.

Give Yourself Some Love

If you're anything like I was years ago, it's hard to start loving yourself out of the blue, and you might not know where to begin. It may take regular acts of self-care to bring that affectionate feeling out in a way that authentically impacts your vibrational field. To practice self-love, I like to start with the basics. So far, you've become more in touch with yourself—increasingly aware of what you think, feel, and want—which means you're ready to nourish yourself in elemental ways. Begin with foundational self-love efforts like sound nutrition, spiritual fulfillment, proper rest, intimacy, and healthy social interactions. These habits will bloom offshoots like cooking, napping, snuggle sessions, throwing fun dinner parties, meditating, and seeing friends. Self-care is about doing what it takes to feel good and hold yourself in high esteem, and then doing it as often as you need to lift your mood and energy. It is a remarkable gift that you can repeatedly give yourself, and it never gets old, especially when you have multiple options at your disposal.

Much like with pattern interrupts, figuring out which self-care activities work best for you is so personal. Be creative, and if one activity doesn't move you, try another! Think about what you feel naturally inspired to do—maybe try a yoga video, see a movie, cuddle under a blanket—and let your intuition guide you. One of my favorite self-love activities is creating a love board. This is similar to a vision board, except here, you tack up pictures from your past and present that remind you of all the people, places, and things that you love about your life and yourself. These might include family photos, images of your home, holiday meals, pets, and other symbols of achievement, affection, joy, and peace. Love boards are powerful reminders that so much of what appears in front of you is the result of manifesting on a frequency generated by love. On my own love board, I have photos from my workshops, of my husband and kids, of me on a mountaintop, of paintings from grateful clients, and of the kids we've philanthropically helped in the Philippines. Surrounding myself with these images of love reminds me of how lucky I am to serve others and makes me feel worthy of giving love to myself too.

Another popular activity that initiates self-love in my clients is to do a self-care activity from childhood, which is when your energy was at its most light and pure. Such activities could include walking barefoot in the cool grass, riding a bike in a cul-de-sac, and dunking Oreos in milk while watching your favorite sitcom. When I was seven years old, I used to make myself a cup of decaf tea, dangle my feet in the pool in my mother's backyard, and talk to God about anything and everything. I'd pray for friends, thank God for my life, and have a little chat about what was going on around me. I still do this today as a self-love activity and to tap back into the innocence and love that I felt when I was young, so I can embody it now.

The Power of Love Energy

Every one of us has a large and dominant energy field that sends out most of the frequencies that communicate with the world around us—but within that larger field, there are smaller fields that con- tribute to the collective whole. Believe it or not, your heart's energy field and frequency output is much stronger than that of your brain, whose energy is smaller and denser. This is why, despite how much I focus on strengthening and building healthy neuropathways, it's equally important to drop into your heart space when manifesting. And because love frequency is so powerful in general, this is why the heart's energetic field can also be used to encourage healing.

When I worked with patients in a Norway clinic, I'll never for- get counseling a Lithuanian woman who was kidnapped as a teen- ager and then brutally raped in the woods. She'd come to us with serious heart problems, to the extent that this organ was shutting down. The woman spoke no English, so we worked with a trans- lator, and there were cultural differences to overcome as well; this meant that the majority of the love that the patient felt would need to be viscerally experienced rather than heard or interpreted to impact our sessions together. Initially, I assumed that the woman's heart condition might have been caused by her rape, but she in- sisted that she underwent 10 months of intense therapy to process her feelings, and after my own evaluation, she did seem well to me. So my research team and I moved on to using a molecular spec- troscopy machine, developed by a governmental institute in Mos- cow and used in hospitals throughout the world. This instrument reads molecular movements and interprets the frequency pattern of the movements; it was able to tell us what was happening in every part of the patient's body on a very granular level—from the woman's organs to her intestinal fluid. This machine confirmed that the health issue in this patient was in fact psychosomatic in nature due to the frequency pattern that the machine reported, so our next step was to then attach her to another instrument, which resembles a souped-up biofeedback machine; this gave us further insight into her condition and it registered that sure enough, there was no trauma substantially affecting her heart that was related to her rape. Even so, we knew that her problem was caused by some kind of internal conflict or stress and that her heart's energy field was malfunctioning.

It wasn't until I asked the woman about her mother (based on a random instinct that spoke to me) that we got to her issue's root cause: she told me that her mom was dying from a terminal disease, and the machine indicated that this was in fact the source of the woman's heart condition. From there, I counseled the woman for roughly four hours, based on intuitive hits that I received during the process, exuding as much love as I could. I used my own heart's energy field to try to affect hers. I intuited that this woman felt that her mother was the only form of unconditional love she ever knew, and that she'd told herself unconsciously that she would rather die than live without that love. Consequently, her subconscious developed a health condition, in her heart of all places, that would guarantee her end—the subconscious reel she'd actually manifested. In other words, the woman unknowingly willed her heart to shut down, her energetic field complied, and the machine confirmed this reality. Once I could lovingly convince her that there was real love to be found outside her mom and show her that it was important and possible to practice self-love once she left the clinic, the energy field around her heart began to respond, and the machine later showed a shift in her brain's ability to accept this possibility. I realize that the patient's diagnosis and healing required a leap of faith, but according to the brain feedback shared with me, there was no argument that we'd hit upon the true cause and solution to the patient's problems.

Learning to identify, replicate, and cleverly utilize the frequency of love is everything. You'll know you're on a love frequency because your own energy will feel light and easy; mentally, you'll be in the now and not thinking about any negativity from the past or anything that might crop up in the future. You might feel and recognize this love frequency when you play with your kids, catch of whiff of freshly baked cookies, or watch the sun rise while sipping an iced tea like your grandma used to make. If you're feeling a lack of self-love, it helps to tap into these kinds of positive memories as well as your imagination. If I can't find love within myself for some reason, I like to close my eyes and remember what it's like to feel my husband's, God's, or my own love that I give to others. I imagine pulling that energy inward, toward my heart, and then pumping it out into my energy field. This way, I bring love to everything I do.

Because your feelings influence the energy that you put out into the world, which affects the life you inevitably manifest, stay on top of what you're telling yourself about love and self-love. In your journal, feel free to explore how you define self-love, what it makes you feel, and why you feel that way. Knowing the difference between good and bad notions of self-love is essential. Those who live in true love are so at peace that they can create and manifest with great ease. We place so many conditions on self-love that aren't necessary or true since so much of how we define and demonstrate love in general is based on programming. Once you know what your subconscious reel calls love, you can redefine these false notions so that they more accurately reflect the kind of love you wish to receive and give. Learning how to pursue all things with love and self-love is just one kind of intentional energy that helps manifestations come true.

Tips and Takeaways

+ Love is a high-frequency emotion and highly memorable feeling. When you feel unconditionally accepted and cared for, your desire to protect yourself from triggers and personas breaks down.

+ Those who refuse or don't feel love act in ways that stem from scarcity, inauthenticity, and loss.

+ Self-love fuels limitless potential. It puts you on a high vibration where limitless creation is possible; it lets you dream about what you want *and* believe you're worthy to receive it.

+ When your life doesn't look the way you'd like, you take love away from yourself—despite the fact that love is one of the most powerful frequencies that lets you create what you want.

+ Self-care counteracts programming and teaches you what it is to feel and give true potent love.

+ God is the ultimate source of unconditional love. God is in all things and everywhere, which means that no matter how the world lets you down, you're still surrounded by God's love.

+ Self-love helps you show up in the world as someone who speaks and lives their truth.

+ Your heart's energy field and frequency output is much stronger than your brain's.

✦ On a love frequency, your own energy feels light and easy; mentally, you're in the now and not thinking about any negativity from the past or anything that might crop up in the future.

More Resources and Free Downloads

If you enjoyed this chapter, I've put together a downloadable pdf called *"Affirmations For Self-Love"* where I share some of my most powerful affirmations you can use daily to remove all blocks to love and self-love. Download it for free at www.authenticliving.com/gifts

Chapter 8

Secret #5

EMBRACE INTENTIONAL ENERGY *to* START MANIFESTING

One of the most underrated, misunderstood, and divinely essential keys to manifesting any goal is your ability to harness the best intentional energy that will set actual manifestation steps in motion. Not surprisingly, this must be energy that's true, light, and good versus that which carries a denser frequency caused by negative emotions like obligation, guilt, or unhealthy love and connection. The right intentional energy should also strike a crucial balance: it should feel deeply invested in, yet simultaneously detached from, the outcome that you desire. When you embrace and emit the right kind of intentional energy, it's like choosing your route at a fork in the road: you can opt for a smooth path that

gets you to your destination quickly and easily or a rocky one lit-
tered with potholes and roadblocks. The decision seems obvious
enough, right?

Even so, a lot of manifesters don't know how to find and follow
the smooth road to their final stop. Instead, they bump along on a
precarious path, largely with the assumption that having positive
intentional energy when manifesting means being a good person
when you set a goal, feeling upbeat as you pursue that aim, and/or
choosing a desire that helps others. And while these are lovely values that I highly encourage, I consistently channel that having positive intentional energy around a manifestation is more systematic
and psychological than all of this. It's about embodying a frequency
that ranks above "neutrality" on the emotional/vibrational ladder,
which helps you to reach a goal that fulfills a certain emotional
state. This is what creates the high vibe that brings goals to fruition
and, when you build on this energy, allows you to sustain a high,
dominant frequency for future manifestations and wonderfully unexpected and fortunate events.

You've done so much work to clear your past programming plus
raise your lower vibrations, which can get in the way of feeling the
emotions that spark positive manifestations. Your energy field is
primed for high-intentioned goals to take hold in the purest way,
and you also know how to recognize, and what to do if you sense,
other triggers that create low energy that's inhospitable to manifesting. In other words, you are already in the best possible spot to
create the kind of intentional energy that lets you set amazing goals
and marvel when they come to life. Again, this puts you a giant leap
ahead of most manifesters who may be unknowingly held back by
programming that causes dense and low-frequency tangles in their
fields. A person's positive intention can encourage a manifestation
to come true, but on its own, won't lead to smooth sailing during
the process or when you receive it. The end result could come with

issues: it could be short-lived, or a logistical concern could keep you from enjoying it.

Intentional energy, then, is not about being a certain kind of person or creating specific types of positive goals for manifesting but about embodying the purest energy to back the actions and emotional state that you desire; these keep us in alignment with the universe's highest good and help us avoid the backlash of lower vibrational choices, like those I just mentioned. In this chapter, I'll explain the importance of having the right intentional energy, how to create positive intentions that spark the best manifesting goals, and how to manifest when upsetting life events stand in your way. I'll also outline how to use intentional energy to set and then follow through with your first of many manifesting goals. Having the right intentional energy is a game changer! Let's unlock secret #5 for powerful manifesting.

Understanding Intentional Energy

Let's start with the basics: so what is intentional energy? To put it simply, this is the energetic, driving force behind everything that you do and claim to want. It is the power that directs the movement of particles to be made manifest. Intentional energy is also born from the emotional and mental state that represents your commitment to carrying out an action, now or in the future. As you know, there's always an energy behind your beliefs, emotions, thoughts, and words—so if you want to manifest from a high vibration, you'll need to ignite it with a high-frequency intention first. Eventually, you'll come to sustain a high vibration so that your dominant frequency is consistently elevated, and that's the state in which beautiful, random things are drawn to your auric field. But for now, when it comes to manifesting a goal, the initial key to it all is genuinely positive intentional energy.

Identifying your intentional energy is pretty simple. When you determine the goal that you'd like to set, the feelings that motivate this will feel either good (light and happy) or bad (dense and heavy). Good energy is often rooted in feelings of self-love, possibility, joy, and peace, whereas negative energy comes from feelings like anger, pride, grief, apathy, guilt, shame, fear, obligation, and scarcity. If your intentional energy needs a lift, return to Chapter 6 where I discussed the emotional/vibrational ladder to identify where your feelings currently are on the ladder and which emotions are above it so that you can strive for them. It's usually enough to do a few of your favorite self-love and pattern interrupt exercises to move this needle—for me, a cup of tea and journal entry usually do the trick—but if you still feel stuck after, then it's time to check in and detangle some programming. And remember, you don't have to zoom to the top of the emotional/vibrational hierarchy to create an acceptable intentional energy; bumping yourself up by just a feeling or two, always above neutrality, will boost manifestation odds. Of course, the higher you are on the scale, the faster your outcome will occur since energy moves more quickly as your vibration rises. But there is no timeline for how fast you must learn to climb this ranking; just know that the higher you go, the better it is.

Positive, sustainable manifesting outcomes are directly tied to the right intentional energy. If you hope to manifest success, your intentions behind this goal should be genuine and for the highest good of all. Wanting to do well at work because you were bullied as a kid that created a deep-seated anger that made you want to prove everyone wrong so that you'd never be made fun of again? This is not of the highest good. A long-standing frustration doesn't even rank above neutrality. Sometimes these low vibrations won't allow anything to happen, or a manifestation will come to pass but in a less than ideal scenario. You might get that promotion or raise, but you'll feel burned out, you'll get a bill in the mail that eats up your extra salary, or your new position will be eliminated shortly after you've taken it. This is because the energy around your actions and outcomes is denser when your intentional energy springs from low desires. On the other hand, doing well at work so that you can provide an exciting, comfortable, and carefree life for you and your family will put you on the right positive frequency for consistent and long-lasting success. You'll thrive in the new post, watch the money naturally flow in, and feel divinely guided the whole time. Point blank: when you change your energy, you change the outcome of your manifestation. Your action doesn't have to alter, but your intentional energy should. You can see how working through your most obvious programming before you start to manifest, and then as you encounter triggers during the manifestation process and daily life, is so necessary. Preemptive measures allow you to feel prepared plus be proactive versus reactive.

It's worth repeating that because you've done so much psychological work so far, you have a better chance of automatically having higher intentions and a purer energy flow around your goals. Yay, you! Manifesting from a pure, clean state versus one of fear and programming pulls you out of the past and what no longer has to exist, and thrusts you into the now, where possibilities are endless. Your ability to zero in on what you want, and why you want it, should be more acute too. But what I also find is that when my clients begin to manifest, they may think that they want to achieve a certain thing—like being successful—but after checking in and untangling their energy and removing blocks as a way of life, they realize that what they thought they wanted all along wasn't a fit after all. In fact, I'll bet that what *you* thought you wanted to manifest when you first picked up this book is shifting and reshaping after having done so much work on your programming. This is a really good thing since your new perspective will help you to manifest from a more authentic, and therefore more effective, vibrational place.

If you think about it, at the heart of what we're all chasing isn't a set of things, but an emotional state that comes from the stuff we strive to attain. So if you're pursuing a tangible goal to reach an emotional state, you may find that in your higher vibration, which comes with mental clarity, you may want to access this emotional state another way and then tweak your manifesting goal. So to use the success example, while you may have once been dead set on manifesting professional success, after all your check-in and detangling work, you may now realize that you were striving for professional accolades because you were actually chasing approval and love. And guess what? You can get that through other means that may feel more fulfilling than a raise and cause you to vibrate higher. You might change your manifestation goal, then, to establishing a charity that pairs bullied children with older classmates to mentor and look out for them, which makes you feel accomplished but also speaks to your need to get accolades from a specific community— and all of this is driven by a passionate, loving intentional energy that radiates high vibrational excitement back into the world. So when you're ready to state a manifesting goal, which we'll do later in this chapter, consider whether the emotional state you seek pairs with your endgame. If not, change it up, because you'll only reach lasting results if your intentions are genuine and vibrating high. And it's easier to get there with goals you're emotionally drawn to versus those that come from worldly or false values.

Finally, having the right intentional energy requires being detached from the outcome. Detachment is important to many spiritual and energetic processes, whether it's manifesting, healing, or channeling. Detachment clears the way for the universe to take care of your request by removing you from lower vibrational states like desperation. At first, detachment might sound hard to imagine since I've just insisted that your positive intentions feel joyful, passionate, and full of love. But detachment doesn't mean that you don't feel excited about your goal or care whether it happens. This means you're giving it over to the universe, and then getting out of the way to allow, in perfect timing, for bigger answers to flow through you than your brain might formulate on its own. You must still take action to help your goal occur when opportunities arise, but when you're detached, there's no stress or control around this, which creates density. As you can see, having faith is important here. It demonstrates your willingness to trust a higher power and the highest good of all plus believe that what is meant to show up will and that there's a bigger, universally minded plan for you at work.

Rather than emotionally disconnect, you're sending your emotion driven energy to a pure, divine space that's in flow with God doing God's thing. I had a client named Amber who wanted to manifest her soul mate. Her boyfriend had left her suddenly, without turning back. It made her feel disposable and convinced her that she must be "disgusting" to have been left so carelessly and easily. She no longer believed that the universe wanted her to feel happy. Initially, Amber told me that her intention when manifesting was to feel loved because she was tired of feeling lonely and like she was "getting older, fatter, and uglier by the day." You already know that this kind of intentional energy won't turn out a partner that would ultimately make Amber happy because it was motivated by scarcity, fear, and self-hatred. Her brain and auric field would scan for it, but they wouldn't provide Amber with prospects that gave her the emotional fulfillment she craved. My guess is that Amber would have metaphorically dated her ex or the unhealed parts of a relationship with a family member since her intentional energy sprung from a low vibe that came from programming. So I worked with Amber to see that boosting her energy with two self-love tactics a day, for two weeks, would get her into a higher state and help her realize that she wanted to feel love because she deserved it and wanted to share her life with an equal. She fully detached from the result but now with a strong and renewed faith that God would take care of her and guide her soul mate to her. From there, Amber deeply believed that her perfect partner was out there and that the right intentional energy would bring him forth. Six months later, Amber met a man she's still dating, and they're very happy.

Sustaining Intentional Energy

In a lot of ways, manifestation is not about attracting *what you say that you want* but *what you vibrationally are.* Stop right now and reread that sentence. This means that if you can sustain a high dominant frequency, life in general will begin to feel miraculous, as manifestations happen easier and good things often occur without a concerted effort. This is because your high dominant energy puts you in flow with the universe's highest energy and good for all concerned. Intentional energy is manifestation specific, but when you build your life around this energy so your frequency is consistently high vibe, you don't have to try to raise it as often. After a few years of practice, I live in a dominantly high vibration where manifestations come true but also random, good things show up all the time that are better than I could have deliberately created.

Infusing daily activities with healthy intentional energy is important because it gets you into the habit of naturally doing this for eventual manifestation and also helps you build and maintain a high, dominant frequency. Infusing daily tasks with the right intentional energy is also important to the people around you. Since our bodies are energetic antennas, and we're always receiving and sending out frequencies to others' fields, you can positively impact anyone in your midst—and you should. This is why a number of addicts that I've worked with have told me that they feel there's a cap to healing through support groups and in no time, found that they'd "outgrown" them. These groups can help you stop drinking or doing drugs, plus build a foundation for growth, but since members often struggle and consider themselves to be lifelong addicts, the overall vibration of the group fluctuates too much for one to evolve and manifest long-term. You might be better off working one-on-one with a counselor, cherry-picking like-minded friends for support, and pursuing a spiritual program like Authentic Living for growth.

Like so many, I've struggled with having an unhealthy, almost addictive attitude toward exercise for much of my life, which has made my intentional energy around this otherwise healthy activity sometimes dubious at best. As a teenager, I was weight-obsessed and bulimic, so for me, exercise always came with the intention of self-loathing. For years after I healed this, I worked really hard to sculpt a beautiful body in a sane way, end my neurotic eating habits, and nourish myself with foods that didn't encourage or trigger binging. Cut to six years later, when my husband and I moved from Dallas to Laguna Beach. The sunny beach-body locale inspired me to get super fit, so I hired a hard-core trainer with an insane body, who put me on an extremely strict regime. I'll bet you can guess what happened next! My allegiance to the trainer and drive to perfect my looks triggered an old version of me, a persona, to come out.

One afternoon while training, I remember struggling to finish a set of squats when I heard a clear voice in my head say, "I hate myself"—and that's what motivated me to complete the last squat! Immediately, without even having to check in, I realized that negative intentional energy had come back to roost because I had a programmed association between intense exercise and negative intentions that motivated me to complete it. I even began to severely break out—an issue that I hadn't experienced since the last time I exercised with this kind of self-loathing energy. Well, that was that. I quit my intense routine immediately and began exercising in a way that was motivated by being healthy, living a long time for my kids, and enjoying food and loving myself enough to embrace that. I still exercise, but my intentional energy doesn't revolve around hating myself or looking good to gain others' approval. Perhaps the most interesting part of this lesson is that I still see fabulous results from my pared-back routine because my positive, high intentions allow me to access an outcome that's even better than if I'd tried to reach it through negative means. The result isn't just more emotionally supportive and fulfilling but equally effective on a physical level too. Changing my intentional energy also lets me leave my home gym on a higher vibrational note that I can carry into everything else I do that day.

As I've mentioned before, sustaining a high vibration doesn't always require check-ins, detangling work, and the like, every time you encounter a trigger—especially if it's situational. Sometimes, it's enough to use a pattern interrupt or self-love activity when you notice that your intentional energy is off. For example, cooking dinner for your family may feel more like an obligation than a gift, and so it lowers your dominant energy just anticipating it, much less doing it. But you can overcome this energetic weight by rewarding yourself with a self-love activity before, during, or after the experience—perhaps by taking a salt bath after you prep the meal, listening to music while you combine the ingredients, or dancing around the kitchen with your kids as you clean up. Here, you must 1) become aware that you don't love what you're doing and then 2) insert a practice that you *do* love into the experience. Voilà— vibration boosted.

Shifting your intentional energy to sustain a high vibration is possible, even when you feel understandably resistant. During my first winter in Colorado, I was shocked at how much snow we got over a few months—especially having hailed from Arizona, Florida, and Texas. Yet despite all the snow, our rescue dog Tank continued pooping out back—and I'm sorry to say, our scooping it up fell by the wayside. Now no matter what the weather is, it's my son Braydon's job to do this gross chore, but those chilly days were daunting, and so we let it go. When the sun came back out and the snow finally melted, you can imagine what the dog run looked like!

When I first saw all that poop, I felt compelled to help Braydon with his monumental task to just get the clean-up done, but my intentional energy was initially one of annoyance and overwhelm. I didn't have a tangled history around shoveling dog poop, so instead of checking in, I did a pattern interrupt to shift the intentional energy around this event so that the higher vibration could feed my own energy and influence Braydon's. I decided that we'd each take up a shovel and laugh our way through this icky activity; appealing to a 10-year-old's sense of humor (and let's face it, my own!), I made poop jokes throughout the process. At one point, the poop even got on Braydon's shoe, and we laughed like crazy. My intentional energy seamlessly transformed to love. Both of our frequencies were elevated as a result, whereas it could have easily ruined our afternoon! Note that we didn't change our actions around the activity—I didn't hire someone else to do the job or convince my husband to shovel for us. But I did change my intentional energy until the outcome became effortless, efficient, and fun. Always keep in the mind that energy shifts are a choice. You can decide when to do this, and that's empowering!

Pro tip: When you're in a high vibrational state, this is a great time to manifest your heart out and take advantage of having naturally arrived at an abundant frequency. In other words, you don't have to start the manifestation process with a goal in mind; sometimes, I begin with a good mood and then come up with one or as many goals as I can while I ride out the high vibe. This way, I don't have to work too hard at creating positive intentional energy; it's already flowing in the right direction. To this point, as soon as I was done shoveling a month's worth of poop with my son, I ran inside and set a few manifesting intentions into action—a process I'll explain next.

Ready to Manifest? Let's Do This!

Learning to harness positive, intentional energy is actually the first manifestation step you'll take toward realizing your goals. Until now, you've paved the road for a clear mind and high, dominant vibration. And now, it's time to learn how to execute the steps to manifestation! Though I talk a lot about manifesting big dreams like professional success, wealth, finding your soul mate, and buying your dream home, my clients also like to manifest everyday goals like taking a great trip, losing weight, and even finding the best new coffee maker. After all, once you exist on a high, dominant vibration all the time, manifesting just becomes a way of life. It's a tactic you can use to acquire *anything* you desire, no matter how important or trivial it seems.

Step 1

First, I'd like you to identify one goal that you'd like to manifest and be sure the intentional energy behind it is pure and high. You can do this by checking to see how the energy feels in your body when you consider it, or by asking yourself, *Why do I want this?* If your answer is positive and feels light, then you can move to the next step. If it feels burdened or heavy, it's time to check in and detangle the energy around your manifestation goal, and then get to a higher vibration through this process and by using pattern interrupts and self-love techniques as needed. That being said, the reason for low intentional energy doesn't *have* to date back to past programming or trauma; your intentional energy may feel less than ideal, based on, say, crummy stuff going on that day, in which case, all you truly need is to figure out a self-love or pattern interrupt activity to lift your spirits. Either way, determining your "why" doesn't have to be a lot of work, and however you raise your energy is well worth the time you devote to it since you'll have a better manifesting outcome and build a higher dominant frequency over time. Can you remember the last time you were in a high vibe, and how amazing that felt? Get there again! Once you do, your intentional energy will shift or you may choose to change your goal to one that matches the emotional state you're hoping to achieve, which puts you on a higher, more genuine vibration. Know, too, that it's always better to use your energy to keep yourself in a high state than allow yourself to get into a really low state and then pull yourself up from there. Think of it like swimming: it's easier to paddle downstream than up, right?

Step 2

After identifying the goal that matches the emotional aim you're trying to reach, you're going to journal. I want you to write at the top of the page, "I'm in the process of ___,"—and then state your manifestation goal. I don't like to state future goals from an "I am" perspective—as in, "I am healthy" or "I am in love"—because it can feel disingenuous or silly, and the mind will tell you it's not true, which lowers your vibration since the goal feels unobtainable. But writing, "I'm in the process of falling in love" or "I'm getting healthier every day" is a statement that your mind can get on board with. This is one of the few times that I'm going to ask you to watch your words. I don't believe that you need to speak with positive language as you go about your whole day because by now you know it's the energy behind your words that is most important. Think about it: you can say "I love you" with many types of intentional energy—sincerity, frustration, apathy, passion—and this frequency is what you should always stay on top of.

Step 3

Get specific and list out any relevant details attached to your goal. If you're aiming to manifest a soul mate, what does that person look like? What's his or her character? Important personality traits? How does it feel when you're together? Then attach a deadline for your goal. Write, "I'd like to achieve this by ___." Finally, draw the manifestation. You don't have to channel Pierre-Auguste Renoir, here; elementary stick figures and line drawings are great! Be as simple or elaborate as you want, so long as the image conjures joy and love. By the end of the exercise, you should feel really excited, energized, and enthusiastic about reaching this goal!

Step 4

Next you're going to do a visualization exercise for up to 15 minutes. After working with thousands of clients, and manifesting an incredible life for myself, I've found that the most effective visualizing happens when you're in a half-sleep—so, either when you're drifting off to la-la land, a state referred to as "hypnagogic," or transitioning from sleep to wakefulness, which is a "hypnopompic" state. Personally, I like to refer to either period as "manifestation hour." The moment you're either aware that you're drifting to sleep or waking up from it is when you will restate the intention you wrote in your journal. Then, visualize what it feels like to either go through the process of pursuing your goal or how it feels to reach it—whichever is most thrilling and high vibe to you. It might even help to imagine yourself in a scene from your final goal—perhaps buying a new car when you manifest millions or stretching to run a marathon when your arthritis heals. Play around with this mental image until you're using as many of your five senses as you can to visualize your endgame. Be sure the emotional state you embody matches the one that you're trying to achieve with the manifestation.

Let's briefly talk about the two manifestation half-sleep states, because they're super interesting, and you'll want to decide which one is most comfortable and natural for you. One state is not necessarily better than the other; like so many details in the manifesting process, it's really a matter of preference. During a hypnagogic state, your imagination is on fire. Your intuition links memories and concepts through feelings of familiarity and sensed associations. Creative solutions bubble to the surface. No wonder it's so common to have involuntary experiences like hallucinations, lucid dreaming, and even sleep paralysis during this sleep state.

Because the brain is so ripe for creation during a hypnagogic state, many scientists, musicians, authors, and artists have used this for inspiration and problem solving. Mary Shelley's book *Frankenstein*, for instance, was inspired by a hypnagogic dream. Reportedly, scientist Thomas Edison would deliberately lie on his sofa to go to sleep while holding a spoon or two steel balls over the edge and above a plate. The moment he'd drift off, he'd drop the objects. The loud crash would then wake him up—and before Edison forgot the ideas and insights he had during his hypnagogic state, he'd write them all down. Artist Salvador Dalí, who used hypnagogic dreams as inspiration for his surrealist paintings, used a similar technique but with a heavy key that he'd drop onto a plate while falling asleep. According to one scientific journal, between 39 to 85 percent of people experience this "dreaming," so if you're game to visualize with a spoon or key in hand, I believe that it's a very powerful opportunity to co-create with the universe.

A hypnopompic state is the opposite of a hypnagogic one, and what I prefer to use while manifesting a specific goal. Doing this practice first thing in the morning is easiest; plus, it begins your day with an elevated vibration, which starts you off on the right foot. You can also do it when you're waking up from a nap. Either way you're relaxed, mostly awake, and mentally coasting. You're more aware of being in between two states at once than during a hypnagogic state; you can recognize what's on your mind or what you were dreaming while asleep, while also thinking about your day ahead. I think this transitional state works so well because your brain hasn't fully turned on yet, and so past programming hasn't begun to affect your thoughts. The process reminds me of how a channeler detaches from her mental state to receive messages and allow energy to flow through her. With your cognizant mind out of the way yet still receptive to imaginative creations, you can insert your visualizations.

Step 5

Now that you've set your manifestation the night before or that morning, enjoy going about your day in a lighter, clearer headspace. Detach from your goal but continue to check in with yourself if you feel triggered so that you can do what's needed to sustain a high vibration.

Feel free to review the five manifestation steps as often as you need to remind yourself how to harness powerful intentional energy. Next I'll illustrate how the process plays out, from beginning to end, with an example from my own life. This way, you can see how one step seamlessly leads to the next. So, I recently manifested one heck of a dream home for my family. When we moved to Colorado from California, we temporarily lived in our retreat center, and it was not ideal. I wanted everyone in my family to have their own space, free from clients' energetic purging and healing processes. I also wanted my kids to have a magical place to call home. Now a great house kept popping in and out of my awareness, but it cost more than I wanted to spend, so I kept it in mind but mostly blew it off. I'd briefly met the owner at a charity event, and while I loved the space, it needed work, and again, I didn't like the price. Even so, I couldn't shake the intuitive feeling that if the conditions were right, this would make a great forever home for our clan.

I grabbed my journal and wrote the intention "I am in the process of moving," drew a photo of the home as I wanted it to look, and listed specifics like the cost and other details that would make it a perfect fit. I then restated my intention and visualized during my hypnopompic state every morning and approached it with high intentional energy, helped along by imagining my kids playing in the yard, my husband reading in the library, our family gathering for movie nights on the sofa, and me, making dinner in the kitchen while looking at the snowcapped mountains. I used as many of my senses as I could, imagining how it felt when the sun hit my face on the property or how it smelled with adobo cooking on the stovetop (one of my family's favorite dishes). After 15 minutes or so, I released my goal with the highest good for all and detached from it (some refer to this as "let go and let God"—the energy is similarly nonchalant). Within *one week* only, the house's owner knocked on my door and offered us his home, with the exact price I'd manifested and with no input from me! Isn't that incredible? It was practically served up on a gilded plate. We moved into the house five weeks later, and it is the gift that keeps on giving: a warm, loving space for my family to thrive.

When you're new to manifesting, I suggest starting with just one manifestation goal at a time until the universe starts delivering action steps for you to take en route to your destination. I'll talk more specifically about these in the next chapter, but for now, I want you to see how they fit in with the whole manifestation process. With action steps, you'll follow them almost like bread crumbs on a path until you reach your tangible and emotional goals. For instance, after the homeowner knocked on my door, I took the steps to proactively negotiate the rest of our agreement until our contract was settled, and then obviously packed up our stuff, scheduled the movers, and so on. The universe had already signaled it was go-time when I heard the prior owner's knock; now it was time for me to do *my* part. Manifestation isn't just a mental and energetic process; it involves some *doing* to get you to the finish line because we live in a 3D world, and you can't expect the universe to take care of every detail. I also see action steps as a sign that the wheels are firmly in motion on your first goal, and that you can progress to others. If manifesting multiple goals at once, it may help to compartmentalize these into different categories like health, love, family, money, a new home, and so on. Should categories present obstacles, untangling only a few unrelated ones is easier than juggling many that tend to overlap.

Hit a Manifesting Roadblock? No Problem!

Not every route to your manifestation goal, of course, will be smooth sailing. Sometimes in the midst of manifesting, life happens to us—and when obstacles present themselves, we have to either work with them or navigate around them. Situations like a sudden trauma, death in the family, abuse, illness, divorce, or other unexpected events make it hard to sustain high-level emotions. And if the experience is recent, it might take a while to heal, and that's out of your hands. Don't worry—this is fine. Even normal! The universe is always looking out for you. Have faith in God's plan.

Should you encounter a roadblock, your dominant frequency may be low, but your intentional energy behind a manifestation goal can still be inspired and high enough to co-create—especially if you've untangled a lot of your past programming already with check-ins and detangling exercises. Remember, your frequency only needs to vibrate above a neutral feeling. Typically, self-love and pattern interrupts can get you there, even when times are hard. This makes me think of my friend Marie who was incredibly sick from Lyme disease, which was ruining both her health and her relationship with her family. Even so, she somehow managed, from this incredibly dense state, to write a book that helped others to cope with their own difficult illnesses. Though at times Marie felt like she could hardly push through another day, she managed to create something beautiful and successful even when her dominant vibration didn't necessarily support it. I believe that part of this was God throwing her a bone, and the rest had to do with having focused, positive intentional energy around her manifestation despite her challenging experiences. To me, it makes sense that God wouldn't allow a bad situation to keep you from doing good work and achieving it in a way that lifts your spirits, your vibration, and has the potential to radiate goodness to others. I believe God's energy wants you to feel inspired, even during the darkest moments, to keep going for yourself and the collective.

Events beyond your control can also interfere with a manifestation before it has a chance to come true, and when this happens, I believe that it means that the universe is steering your life in a different direction than you intended. God always has divine timing in mind, and we must learn to trust it. A new path may still aim toward the emotional state you originally wanted but with a different end result. Trust that this fresh route will lead to the highest good that brings you the most happiness. That said, you may want to tweak your manifestation when life events shift and trust the universe to fill in the gaps. I'm thinking of a client who spent months visualizing a new home with her family, just like I did, when her husband's free will suddenly stepped in and he asked for a divorce out of the blue. This was clearly not what my client expected, much less manifested, and she had to trust that God would meet her emotional goal of fulfillment and family in a different way. I also advised her to stick with her manifestation, but this time, leave the face of her partner blank and create a second manifestation goal of who this person might be. At the time of this writing, her goal had yet to come to pass, but we both have faith that it will.

Manifesting with the right intentional energy is both imperative and fulfilling. It not only effectively brings goals to fruition but also makes you feel amazing while doing it. Now that you're clear on how to set a manifestation goal with the highest energy you can muster, let's make sure that the path is clear for you to take the best action steps and deal with perceived hiccups along the way.

Tips and Takeaways

✦ Intentional energy is the driving force behind everything you do and claim to want. It directs the movement of particles to be made manifest. Intentional energy is also born from the emotional and mental state that represents your commitment to carrying out an action, now or in the future.

✦ Positive, sustainable manifesting outcomes are directly tied to the right intentional energy.

✦ The energy around your actions/outcomes is denser when intentional energy comes from low desires.

✦ Having the right intentional energy requires being detached from the outcome.

✦ Manifestation is not about attracting *what you say that you want* but *what you vibrationally are.*

✦ Infusing daily activities with healthy intentional energy gets you into the habit of naturally doing this for manifestation and helps you build and maintain a high, dominant frequency.

✦ Start with just one manifestation goal at a time until the universe sends you action steps.

✦ When unexpected events and obstacles interfere with a manifestation, the universe is steering your life in a different direction. Embrace it!

More Resources and Free Downloads

If you enjoyed this chapter, I've put together a guided mediation called "5 Steps to Instant Manifestation" that walks you through the 5 steps I discussed in this chapter. Download it for free at www.authenticliving.com/gifts

Chapter 9

Secret #6

CREATE A
MANIFESTATION
BLUEPRINT
for ACTION STEPS

After setting a manifestation goal into motion, I wouldn't fault you for assuming (or even hoping!) that from here on out, it's simply a waiting game until your dream finds its way to reality. But the truth is the very best manifesters know that it helps to be cleverly proactive during this time. Until you reach the finish line, you should continue visualizing every night or morning after reciting your manifestation statement, stay detached from the outcome during the day, and address any triggers that pop up so that you're always cruising on a high vibration. This may sound a bit complicated if you're thinking this process through with only your headspace, but

I can promise you that after years of doing this myself and with thousands of clients, this procedure will naturally become your way of being—in no time at all. Pattern interrupts and self-love activities, as they're needed, will also help you sustain a dominant, high frequency. The final step in the actual manifestation process, then, is to take action steps toward your goal that are guided by the universe and a manifestation blueprint that adjusts your mindset and helps you navigate triggers that come up as you reach your final destination. This is secret #6: creating and following the steps of your blueprint.

As I briefly mentioned in the last chapter, after you set a manifestation in motion, the universe will send you various signals that your manifestation is coming to life and also point to practical things you can do to help get you where you want to go. Now you won't be pointed toward *every* move you're meant to make, but you will notice guidance that indicates next steps and/or validates the ones you're taking (the universe doesn't hand over all the answers because the learning and discovery process is necessary to the soul's evolutionary journey on earth, which is largely about making choices that lead to growth). So, for instance, if you're manifesting reliable childcare, you might bump into a friend at the market whose nanny is looking for extra work. Or while listening to a podcast, you might hear great advice about budget travel when you're manifesting an epic anniversary trip. And how will you know if a conversation, event, or sudden meeting is meaningful to your action steps? Since you're now vibrating on a higher frequency, your instincts will give you a quiet nudge. You'll think *Oh, this is something*, or *Wow, what a coincidence . . .* If I so much as stub my toe, I view it as feedback from the universe and pay attention to what's happening at that moment to explain why God is getting my attention. I ask myself, *What does this sign mean, and why is God telling me this right now?* Increasing your awareness of signs will speed manifestations too since you're essentially in conversation with the universe when you acknowledge and then follow them toward your goal.

Now you may find that as you plot and take each step, you feel tempted to dip into past programming when either reacting to or determining what comes next—and this is where your manifestation blueprint becomes especially helpful. Figuring out a series of actions is a very methodical, left-brained maneuver, and your programming may be tempted to control and even worry about what's around the corner. When an action step triggers low vibrational feelings stemming mostly from fear—fear of loss, fear of the unknown, fear of rejection, and so on—your blueprint will tell you how to quickly address this block so that you don't have to do a full check-in and detangle unless you have deeper work to do. And you'll know if it's time to dig further because the blueprint techniques will feel too simplistic to detangle your energy. You'll sense that the issue goes much deeper than you first realized and then feel driven to resolve it.

In this chapter, I will illustrate how to create a manifestation blueprint so that you can take your final manifestation steps in the cleanest and most direct way possible. As you enter the homestretch of your manifestation goal, your blueprint will support your action steps so that you can work in tandem with the universe for a result that feels effortless and meant to be. You may encounter what feel like hiccups along the way, but try to view this as feedback that allows you to receive your manifestation in the highest good. Your goal is so close, you can practically feel it!

Drafting a Manifestation Blueprint

For every goal you have, a manifestation blueprint is a must because it helps you carve out the best path to turn hopeful goals into concrete realities. It also helps you figure out how to react to triggers since action steps can introduce you to situations outside your comfort zone. I refer to manifestation blueprints as such because to me, a blueprint is a game plan—a technical design that keeps you on track with your original intentions and desires. Emotions can't sway it, and random mishaps won't throw it off because it was created in a clear state. Your manifestation blueprint, then, will address three main points that will keep you aligned with your manifestation goal: 1) how to create an "expectation mindset" as you take steps toward your goal, 2) how to most effectively take your action steps, and 3) how to respond when a step triggers you so that you can keep your vibration high and not submit to a lower, fear- or programming-based frequency. You don't have to write down your steps, but I find that it helps so you can remove those that feel excessive and cross off the steps you've taken as you do them. You can write this in the same section of your journal where you wrote your manifestation statement and drew its picture.

Create an Expectation Mindset

The crucial first step in creating a great blueprint involves fine-tuning your frame of mind so that your action steps are fueled by *great expectations*. I realize that you've already done, and continue to do, all that you can to sustain a positive vibration. Now I'd like you to make one final, powerful tweak in perspective. I'd like you to consciously decide, without a shadow of a doubt, that your goal is going to occur. The ideal way to do this isn't through self-talk but to adopt the frame of mind that the manifestation is already happening, just as if you'd scheduled it as an upcoming event on your calendar. If you think about what it feels like to, say, make a hair appointment, the moment that you've scheduled the activity and put it in your calendar, your mind becomes relaxed and you trust that it will occur. You don't doubt that it's happening or think of 837 backup plans if it falls through. You don't anticipate an emotional fallout based on a bad past experience or one that's yet to happen. You feel neutral and move on. And if you schedule an event that's more exciting, like a birthday party, you assume a similar expectation mindset but with the added emotional and frequency boost of happiness. In both cases, you vibrate at a neutral level or above as you await a reasonable outcome. Manifesting with the assumption that your goal will occur should feel similar to these examples.

Establishing the expectation that a manifestation is already on its way to you also energetically opens you up to a future that hasn't happened yet and sparks the vibration of possibility. Belief in this possibility moves energy faster because it's motivated by faith and hope or trust, which are positive intentions. Acting as if your goal is already en route also supports a dominant, high vibration. If you act as if your soul mate or healed relationship with your mom are on your doorstep, you'll feel high vibrationally and pull that frequency toward you. Even from a religious point of view, faith and expectation go hand in hand. The Bible says in the book of Isaiah that God is always looking and longing to be good to you, but you have to *expect* God to be gracious first. I'm not a particularly religious person, but I love the underlying truth of this statement.

Though I discouraged you from using "I am" statements while declaring your manifestation statement in the last chapter (because your mind is less likely to accept an affirmation that's more optimistic than realistic), now that you're *combining an expectation mindset with action steps*, your mind will have an easier time believing that any outcome is possible. And when the universe shows you those steps, your mind will be excited to embrace them as positive indicators of what to do next rather than dismiss them as coincidences or view them through the lens of a persona or programming. This reminds me of my client Carmine, a stay-at-home mom whose husband was an out-of-work contractor when we met. And although the family was in such a bad way that they relied on food stamps,

Carmine was able to borrow enough money from her parents to attend my 30-day online program—and based on what she learned, manifest the fee for one of my live events, which unexpectedly appeared in the mail as a delayed tax refund! She also visualized meeting me and my husband at our live event and that our children would play together during a lunch break. Sure enough, this is exactly what happened.

More importantly, Carmine more fully learned at my workshop how to master my eight manifesting secrets, which she began using on a daily basis. Within three months, Carmine's husband was back to work, and they'd dug themselves out of debt. What amazed me when I met Carmine, though, wasn't necessarily her resourcefulness or determination—but her mental conviction and expectation mindset that supported her action steps. She never doubted, for instance, when she received a sign to sell one of their cars to pay down bills or bring her husband to one of my workshops with her so their financial manifesting goals were in sync. From the start, Carmine's laser-focused mind was fully on board with the steps she had to take toward her manifestation goals, and as a result, the money she needed to regain her family's footing arrived without worry.

There are a few practical ways to shift your mind to a state of positive expectation if you find it difficult to do through imagination alone. The first trick asks that you actually don't go so far as to view things as you expect them to be but to see them for how they are in the moment. If you consider a possible outcome without being overly optimistic or pessimistic, you will land in a neutral state, or at least one of willingness, that leans toward possibility—and this gradually paves the way for expectation. After all, if you're in a situation where life feels painful and hard, it might be too much of a leap to expect everything to become wonderful and simple; taking a tiered approach may be easier to mentally digest. I get that. So here, after seeing things as they are, consider if a certain outcome is possible. Ask yourself, *If it's easy to expect my manifestation to go sideways, is it just as possible to expect my manifestation to come true?* Chances are, your mind will agree that it is, and your expectation mindset will follow. For instance, let's say you suffer from the on-going, chronic symptoms of what was once an acute infection. You feel rotten, so let's blatantly admit that. From there, it may be hard to immediately believe that healing is your fate. But if it's easy to expect a lifetime of sickness, is it just as possible to expect a full recovery? Of course it is. From there, you should expect that your improved health is well on its way to you. Our cells' well-being is influenced by energy, including thought energy.

You can also lean on others to help you look forward to the certain arrival of your manifestation outcome. One way to do this is to look for hard proof from others' experiences to show you that your goal is possible. For instance, if you're manifesting a friendly co-parenting relationship with your ex, find someone in a similar situation to yours who's done this just as you'd like to do it. Is there an Instagram influencer who models this relationship or an author who's written about a similar experience to yours? Their behavior, not to mention their energy (even through a book, computer, or phone screen!), could inform your action steps.

When I first began manifesting entrepreneurial success, I watched a lot of interviews with celebrities and motivational speakers on YouTube videos for proof that I could achieve their level of achievement. The videos also helped because they'd illuminate the specific ways these success stories overcame hardships to reach their goals—and this helped me come up with action steps as my mind got on board with the notion that emotional healing and success were possible for me too. Another option is to find an accountability partner to hold you to a higher vibration and expectation mindset during your action steps. This could be a romantic partner, friend, family member, or new and trusted acquaintance—what matters is that they offer a balanced and encouraging perspective as you take your steps. If your accountability partner believes in your goal and expects you and your manifestation to succeed, there's a good chance that you will too. Just connecting with them for a talk or even a walk can act as a pattern interrupt if you need one.

Take Your Action Steps Wisely

Once you're in a state of positive expectation, take the action steps necessary to reach your goal. I like to refer to action steps as the "AMZs of manifesting" because rather than follow linear steps from A to B to C . . . until you arrive at Z, your manifestation blueprint lets you make quantum leaps from A to M to Z, for example. So again, after you've set your manifestation, the universe will send you signs about what your next steps should be, and on their own, these often help you to skip ahead. Signs might include an actionable measure like hearing from an old friend out of the blue who, while you were busy manifesting a nutritionist, happened to be overcoming the same food allergies you have with an integrative dietician. You might also receive validation that you're on the right track, like when you take an action step and then see butterflies outside your bedroom window or notice repeating numbers on your clock that act as a thumbs-up from the universe that things are moving your way.

The AMZ process worked well for a past workshop attendee named Joan, who was a therapist. She treated female trafficking and abuse victims and wanted to manifest a healing retreat center for them. With an expectation mindset, Joan knew her first step was to find seed money for her business, and two days after writing this down, Joan's aunt called. Joan told her about the retreat center, and without missing a beat, her aunt felt so inspired that she offered Joan the exact amount that she needed to start construction. This allowed Joan to skip steps toward her goal, like researching how to get a loan, filling out the necessary paperwork, researching potential investors, and so on.

The AMZ process also worked for a client named Trina, an amazing woman and veteran who wanted to open a bath salt business. She told me that she'd been trying to manifest this for years, and had all the plans, products, and passion in place, but couldn't get herself to the launch. I pulled out my whiteboard and asked Trina what steps she felt she needed to take to make this happen. Trina had roughly 15 steps in mind, some of which would take months to accomplish or funds she didn't yet have. After we had our list, I went through each task and asked, "Why do we need this step? Can we launch without it?" What we ended up with were just three steps that could not be eliminated and a launch date of two weeks later. What a difference! Trina had a purely tactical issue that her perceived blueprint was getting in the way of. So she started her manifestation process over with positive intentional energy and took the three action steps we'd named. Trina's mind and energy really expected this launch to happen now that she'd revised her action plan, and she was up and running on time. I even partnered with her to sell some of her incredibly healing products online!

Managing Interruptions and Triggers

Though the manifestation process can flow smoothly from beginning to end, it's just as possible to find that action steps trigger you in some way. If this happens, shift your mind to neutrality, and view it as feedback from the universe. Then, to avoid the need to do a full check-in and detangling process to reset your thinking and energy, choose one of these two techniques: The first, and easiest, way to respond to a hurdle or trigger is to use a pattern interrupt. If an action step like e-mailing a co-worker doesn't get you the response you'd like, rather than freak out that your manifestation is failing, give up, and go to bed at 5 P.M., force yourself instead to go outside for a brisk walk to raise your vibe. Or if a step like calling an argu-mentative friend to make nice upsets you and you'd typically blow up as a result, take 10 deep breaths instead and remind yourself of that person's best traits. The second way for handling interrup-tions and triggers is to create a blueprint statement that keeps your manifestation on track. In Chapter 2, I suggested you create an um-brella statement that described the life you desire and suggested you return to this statement to hold yourself accountable if you feel yourself deviating from the mantra. Similarly, when you're at a crossroad with action steps, question whether your response aligns with your blueprint statement. For instance, if you want to mani-fest a book deal, your blueprint statement might be "I'm about to lock down a deal that helps others and makes me feel happy"—and if you find that your actions steps aren't in line with this statement, you can replace it with a new step.

When action steps emotionally trigger you or lead to an unex-pected next step, trust that this is not a mistake or nefarious diver-sion but all part of God's larger plan. *Everything that shows up once you've set your manifestation is universal feedback to ensure that your goal arrives on the highest vibration possible.* If you hit a wall while taking steps or feel emotionally thrown off, this is the universe ask-ing you to heal your reaction and the energy around it. When I first launched my company, I manifested that I'd make a certain amount of money with a specific number of clients each month. As one of my initial action steps, I posted about my private services on Facebook and clients poured in. My first effort was a huge success, and so simple, just as I'd manifested. Because this was beyond en-couraging, I felt intuitively drawn to repeat my efforts the following month. This time, however, I faced a series of hurdles, even though I'd expected that I'd have a successful month and take AMZ-style action steps. I bounced from one hotel to the next, rental properties for my workshop kept falling through, and I was running out of money fast. I was so upset and confused. But when I thought about how everything had transpired, I realized that after my first gangbuster month, I'd been pushing down a gnawing fear and anxiety about reaching the clients and income I'd manifested. I sensed that this obstacle felt like it would take more than a pattern interrupt or blueprint to fix. I had some detangling to do.

Sitting in meditation, I checked in and then asked myself, *What's the worst that would happen if I continued to get what I wanted?* Almost immediately, I realized that I was absolutely terrified that if my company thrived, I'd lose my boyfriend, who's now my husband, Oliver. You see, I had it in my head that my own mom's professional drive was a problem in her marriage, and I didn't want to repeat that perceived pattern. In my mind, Oliver was way more important than success, and I believed that I had to choose one or the other. I believed this possibility so ardently, in fact, that I'd put the brakes on all manifestation progress and unconsciously counter-manifested from my subconscious reel. I'd actually caused myself to have a lousy month because my action steps were triggering my past programming in a way that I didn't see coming. After detangling the dense energy around my manifestation, I decided to flip my mindset and add an important action step to my process that would double as a pattern interrupt when I made money: I'd celebrate my success with my husband. So every time a check arrived in the mail, we'd have a date night, take a romantic bath together, go for a drive—basically, spend time together in a way that made me feel closer to him rather than threatened that we'd fall apart. I began to view money as a fulfilling reward rather than a potential problem. The next morning while manifesting, I said to the universe, "You wanted us to come to Sedona, and here we are. Make it abundantly clear that you want me to stay by sending me a place to live and influx of income." Within a few hours, my phone and e-mail were off the hook with six great clients that seemed to drop out of the sky. I found a rental property owned by the nicest landlord, who became a dear friend to me and my husband. After my next event, I brought in the same number of clients and income as that first booming month. My action steps had shined a light on a problem that I needed to heal before delivering my manifestation in the highest good. What initially presented as a problem was really an opportunity for growth and consistent abundance.

When universal feedback impedes the flow of your manifestation, it has the power to change everything. I'm a real mama bear, so manifestations related to growing a family really move me. I've had a number of couples come to me with the hope of getting pregnant, and it's amazing to watch feedback from action steps change their manifestation outcomes. My client Leah, for instance, had three beautiful children via in vitro fertilization (IVF), but when she and her husband tried for a fourth, her age became an issue and their IVF efforts didn't work. Though Leah thought IVF was one of her action steps while manifesting a child, her failed pregnancies turned out to be universal feedback. Leah and I then realized that a recent argument with her mom about the financial implications of growing her family had blocked Leah from having a fourth child. Simply acknowledging this problem, mentally forgiving her mom for sowing further seeds of doubt within Leah, and then shifting to an expectation mindset was enough to bring Leah's manifestation to life—literally, and naturally! Leah immediately became pregnant, without the help of her fertility clinic, and finally has the full family she'd always dreamed of.

The more you manifest, the clearer it becomes that this seemingly magical process is simply a calm and grateful exchange between you and the universe. It's a dialogue that awakens you to past opportunities that beg to be healed and thrilling goals that are yours for the taking. The more you manifest, the less of an effort it becomes. To me, manifesting is a lifestyle. It's simply how I get things done, and with practice plus your fresh perspective, it will be this way for you too. Let's next rewrite the rules you live by (uncover secret #7) so your miracle mindset comes naturally.

Tips and Takeaways

✦ A manifestation blueprint is a game plan—a technical design that keeps you on track with your original intentions and desires. It also helps you figure out how to react to triggers.

✦ After you set a manifestation in motion, the universe will send you signals that your goal is taking shape and also point to practical things you can do to help your goal come to fruition.

✦ You won't be pointed toward *every* move you're meant to make, but you will notice guidance that indicates next steps and/or validates the ones you're taking.

✦ If action steps trigger you, shift to neutrality and view it as feedback from the universe.

✦ Establish the expectation that a manifestation is already on its way. This energetically opens you up to a future that hasn't happened yet and sparks the vibration of possibility. Belief in this possibility moves energy faster because it's motivated by faith and hope or trust, which are positive intentions. Acting as if your goal is already en route supports a dominant, high vibration.

More Resources and Free Downloads

If you enjoyed this chapter, I've put together a downloadable pdf called *"My Manifestation Blueprint."* It's a "fill in the blanks" one page guide you can print. Post in front of your mirror for best results. Download it for free at <u>www.authenticliving.com/gifts</u>

Chapter 10

Secret #7

REWRITE *the*
REMAINING RULES

Have you ever wondered what it's like to experience a life bursting with true happiness, consistent centeredness, and oneness with your highest self? Where, day after day, miracles are the new normal, and you feel excited for what's next because what's next is always awesome?

At this point in our time together, you *know* that all of this is possible because the secrets you've practiced so far have begun changing your life. By having learned to address your triggers and take simple steps to keep your vibration high both during and between manifesting goals, you've created an ever strengthening foundation for an enviable life—one in which your greatest desires are always taking shape. And with so much of the right kind of energetic momentum behind you, random good things will soon begin happening to and for you without having to even make a conscientious effort as well. This is because your energy naturally exists on a higher plane now where serendipitous introductions and opportunities are drawn to you as it's simply become the way of things. It's in this space that I'd like you to revise the remaining, primary rules that you live by but have yet to address through trigger and manifestation work.

Rewriting the rules is one of the final finishing touches on your ability to freely glide through the world as the co-creator of a fulfilling life that makes you proud. However, if you don't address these lingering, inhibiting beliefs, you'll slow down future manifestations and find yourself hitting walls or running in circles to navigate your days. You'd likely end up addressing their related blocks when you're triggered at some point, but in the name of vibing high and light at all times, revamping your rules now gets you proactively closer to the overall energetic state you're striving for. Think of this process like sanding down the wood on a kitchen cabinet to be sure it's smooth from the start rather than risk a splinter from rough inconsistencies later on.

In this chapter, I'll encourage you to evaluate and revise your remaining rules in categories that define your lifestyle—and then test out and update each one, every so often. I love this ongoing exercise since it's an indirect way of supporting future manifestations: You're dynamically addressing and elevating all the beliefs in your life that aren't working for you. When you can recognize, define, and then improve the beliefs that motivate your behavior, you can create whatever you want because you're now pouring your consciousness into areas that are supported by high vibrational beliefs. The brain will always do its best to satisfy the rules that run your show. More enlightened ones give it the best options to choose from.

Some Rules Are Meant to Be Broken

Until you began the practices in this book, you likely didn't realize that you were unconsciously living by a limiting and self-defeating set of rules or beliefs, defined by your past programming. Your actions were mostly subconscious reactions to prior experiences and traumas, which allowed them to neurologically and energetically flourish, feeding an unfulfilled life. You operated from programming designed for self-protection rather than pursuing what you wanted. Because you built a far-reaching reality around those old rules, I'm sure you didn't realize how malleable they were. But rules are quite fluid and meant to evolve as you change and grow. And you should always aim to keep growing, which means your rules will always advance with you.

Now that you've mastered so many of the secrets of great manifesters, you have a novel approach to life, complete with updated boundaries and more empowering beliefs. You've also tweaked a lot of your rules already, through check-ins, detangling, persona work, and the like. In my experience, this means that by now, approximately 75 percent of the rules that you live by have already been adjusted in some way! When you address your remaining, dominant rules, it's easier to activate the energetic domino effect I love so much: When you change beliefs, your energy and brain reflect that, and good things happen all the time because you're living in higher vibrations. Whatever is available on those frequencies becomes easily accessible.

Take a minute to think back on some of the rules that used to unknowingly run your life and how you've managed to change them. You may not have framed your beliefs as bona fide rules, but that's what they are. Perhaps the belief that "I'll never be able to support my family as a single mom" has changed to "I can always afford to take care of myself and my family." Or, a rule once defined as "My relationship is doomed because my partner cheated" has evolved to "My partner and I choose to forgive, be open, and communicate with complete trust." Think of how fast it took, and how good it felt, to watch these rules steer your behavior and co-create a new and better reality. You can imagine how consciously improving your thoughts in a few, remaining areas, then, will round out the full picture of the amazing life that is your birthright.

Decidedly naming and adjusting your rules is crucial because your mind needs mental constructs to work with, a map of parameters that guide you through your time on earth. It's just how the cognitive process works. Because of this, you're going to always create rules, even if they're unconscious, but you can also re-create them and establish new neuropathways since neuroplasticity allows the brain to expand and change too. On a more spiritual level, another way to look at this is that nothing on your soul's journey is meant to be finite, and what a beautiful thing that is! Your mind, body, and spirit are interwoven, you're constantly learning lessons that lead to soul enrichment, and if the universe is always expanding, then so are you. Rewriting rules allows the circumstances of your life to change so you can create an ever-expanding reality for yourself versus a shrinking one. I realize that too much change can feel daunting, but when I'm overwhelmed, I like to tell myself that if certain situations aren't going to be the same forever, rather than have the potential to get worse, it means that they have the equal potential to get better. And when you're living by a high vibrational ethos like this one, you're being your most authentic self and therefore deeply connected to, and in flow with, the universe.

As I mentioned, I like to constantly reassess my rules, always moving into higher vibrational realms and trying never to move backward. When programming dictated your life, you lived by rules that were contradicting what you thought you desired and were working toward. You might have felt like you were doing everything in your power to, say, lose weight, expand your family, or heal your body, but if your underlying rules secretly insisted that you'd always be overweight, that you were clinically infertile, or that your health was permanently broken, then you'd never progress in these areas. It's so much more productive to consciously envision a life that you want for yourself and rewrite the rules that will help you materialize that.

I've made rewriting the rules one of the later secrets of highly effective manifesters because I wanted you to first witness and experience in your own life just how realistic and powerful it is to adjust your beliefs, thoughts, and feelings in a way that allows you to reach your goals and change the overall trajectory of your existence. At this point, you should also be able to more swiftly identify the unconscious, stifling rules that impede your ability to manifest and live in a high-minded way. You're more keenly aware of what it feels like to hit walls and blocks that indicate tangled or dense energy. On top of all this, you're tuned in to how bad it feels to operate from a lack of self-love or low intentional energy plus how to respond to a nagging sense that your goals aren't aligned with your purest beliefs, highest vibrational values, and the highest good for others. In other words, you are in the best position—mentally, neurologically, and spiritually—to clearly examine your life and determine how to make the rest of it work for you.

But First—a Meditation

Before you begin the hands-on, tactical process of examining, revising, and testing your new rules, I'd like you to prime the canvas with a meditation and visualization for the best outcome possible. I suggest practicing this meditation before you begin to revise your remaining rules for the first time, and then every time you tweak an existing rule in the future. This exercise will consistently clear your mind to help you formulate the most fruitful rule for you at that time.

First, close your eyes, take three deep breaths, and imagine yourself in a white room. Visualize a beautifully decorated box sitting on a table in front of you. With a knife, slice all four sides of the box and allow it to gently fall open. Inside the box, you'll notice pieces of paper, perhaps index cards, that each have one rule written on them. To rewrite one or more rules, imagine yourself removing the papers whose rules no longer support you and replacing them with handwritten rules that do. Place your new rules, and those that still work, into a new box or jar that's even more lovely than the one before. Don't be surprised if new rules intuitively appear in your mind's eye as you do this exercise; the universe stands at attention when we meditate on self-growth like this. If you are a very capable and specific visualizer, you may want to imagine that your new rule box looks like a recipe box, with notecards organized by dividers in the various categories you'll determine to address. Removing old notecards and replacing them with new ones in corresponding lifestyle categories can help your mind and the universe's energy to recognize your rules more specifically. Picture the box filling with an abundant, colorful light that streams down from the heavens. The light might be pink, if that feels like a love-related color for you, or blue, which may make you feel strong. There is no "wrong" color here; like some of your rules, colors will come to you intuitively and make you feel at ease. Rest assured that this bright light is coming from a divine source and that it is blessing and helping you enact your new rules. Finally, once you're ready, take a few deep breaths and open your eyes.

Identify, Revise, and Test

When it comes to rewriting rules, you can either do this deliberately as an exercise or organically as you stumble on rules that no longer work—or some comfortable and intuitive combination of both, which is what I do. If you address your rules as an exercise, I encourage you to record your rules in a journal or notebook so that you can refer back to them as needed and also track your growth. On the other hand, if you decide to simply rewrite the doozies as you experience them, you'll know it's time to put pen to paper when you feel you've hit a roadblock, sense heavy or dense energy, or feel like a manifestation or goal is taking too long to materialize.

If you're deliberately revising the rules as an exercise, I'd like you to begin by writing down categories of priorities that are meaningful to you. It might help to think of yourself as a towering, delicious birthday cake and these categories as the ingredients that go into making the recipe both functional and unique. For most of my clients, their categories (or ingredients) are finances, career/success, family relationships, romantic relationships, self-love, purpose work, spirituality, and health—but you should create categories that feel specific to your life. You also don't have to rewrite the rules that are working for you; only those that don't. After figuring out these overarching rules and beliefs, you can then list 1) the dominant rule that you live by for each category and 2) what rule you would like to live by instead. If you can't immediately identify your rule within a category, think about ways that this category isn't going your way and tease out a rule that's led to this type of outcome. So, for instance, under romantic love, you might recognize that far too many of your exes have been insulting narcissists. Perhaps your existing rule, then, is that "love is abusive, controlling, and manipulative." Next, determine what rule you'd like to replace it with. Perhaps, "love is supportive, vulnerable, and authentic."

Now that you know your existing and ideal rules, consider which beliefs you'd like to live by to get from point A to B. It's been my experience that most of us can't just make a huge leap from, say, abusive love to authentic love, so instead, I suggest that you follow gradual rules until you reach your final rule. Taking incremental steps helps to mute any anxiety or fear you might harbor that you'll fail, self-sabotage, experience dashed hopes, and the like—all of which carry a low, dense vibration and go against the point of rewriting your rules in the first place.

To create these intermediate rules, I'd like you to write a new rule for each category either every 90 days or when you intuitively sense that an old rule feels heavy or is no longer supporting your happiness. Your new rule, of course, should feel light and inspiring. With each rule that you create, you will then live by that new rule, testing it out in as many natural circumstances as you can to be sure that it's effective. If it isn't, scrap the rule and try again. As with so many other tenets in this book, you don't want to force yourself to practice an unhelpful rule because this will push against the mind's natural inclinations and slow the frequencies that it gives off. If your new rule does bring about the outcome you desire, then you'll stick with it until your 90 days are up or the rule feels heavy and begs to be rewritten. Then, when it's time to rewrite *that* rule, you'll create another fresh rule and keep the process going. Got it?

There is no limit to how many rules or steps it takes to get to your ideal rule. You can write as many rules between your original and ideal rules as you'd like. You might even want to tweak your final rule when you arrive at it, and that's great. Your new rules fuel personal growth, and with that comes fresh insight as to how you'd like to add meaning and fulfilment to your future. For some categories, you might never even have an ideal, final rule. You might choose to keep adjusting your rules as life hums along and your priorities and lifestyle shift over time.

So to continue with the love rule example, after recognizing that your old, counterproductive rule around romantic love is that "love is abusive, controlling, and manipulative," your new rule might be "I admit this isn't love, and when I encounter a situation that feels like love, I'll question whether it's abusive, controlling, and manipulative." From there, you might revise the rule to say, "If I feel unhealthy forms of love, I won't allow myself to experience them. I'll talk to my partner about healing the pattern or choose to leave." See how much closer you're getting to finding a love that's "support-ive, vulnerable, and authentic," which is your ideal rule? Baby steps in the right, positive direction make practicing your rules a breeze.

When it comes to some categories, like career and finances, your rules might be less emotional and more tangible. The more specific you can make a rule, the easier it will be for your mind to carry out and for the universe's energy to match it. An old rule around career success might be "I have to work 12 hours a day and have no family life to make $200,000 a year," which could lead to "I can have a family and work eight hours a day to make $200,000 a year," and eventually, "I can work when I want, and make as much money as I choose because time doesn't automatically equate to success. I can also have an incredible relationship with my children and spouse." As you modify your rules, you will gradually embody the values and goals that you're naming—all while creating an expectation mindset and belief in a positive outcome that energetically paves the way for chance meetings and regular miracles to occur.

Because we all live in a 3D world, our rules don't exist in an ex-clusive, woo-woo spiritual vacuum. We're not always meant to sim-ply make a rule, declare it to the universe, and then wait for God to drop good stuff in our laps around the clock. It might happen this way sometimes, but just as often, as with the action steps associated with manifestations, your higher vibration can be one piece of a larger and more proactive puzzle. When I worked with patients suffering from psychosomatic illnesses, I met a young woman in her 20s named Chanel who suffered from severe nerve damage in her back from having fallen off a horse. One of the first things she said to me was that all her doctors and practitioners—from neu-rologists to physical therapists, to acupuncturists, to chiropractors, and beyond—had insisted that her injury was incurable and as a result, she no longer had faith in the medical world's ability to heal her. The first thing I did, then, was introduce her to a scientist who, in very clinical terms, explained that with the right tools, Chanel's back could repair itself when her cells were given the right electrical stimulation. He went on to explain that, in fact, pulsed magnetic fields from certain devices proved to influence biochemical reactions on a cellular basis. As this expert spoke, I watched Chanel's face and body language transform from one of stubbornness and defeat to one of acceptance and hope. This was my cue to help Chanel create a life-changing new rule.

I could see how Chanel's futile, old rule or belief "I can't heal and doctors can't help me" had already shifted to "I believe healing is possible in the right environment." And as she embraced how this could dramatically improve her body's repair, the doctor prepared to use a papimi, a revolutionary medical device also known as electrically pulsating magnetic field therapy, which induces high-frequency, pulsed, electromagnetic oscillation. The machine never makes direct contact with the body, but its voltage is able to influence the energy balance of mitochondria, which elevates healing potential on a cellular level. After just a few sessions with this technology and a few other therapies, I was told that Chanel regained significant feeling in her back where she'd previously felt nothing—a remarkable healing effect given the extent of her damage! I believe that because Chanel's new rule made it possible for her mind and energy to embrace a positive outcome, her body was even more receptive to changing course.

Drafting Your Rules

As I'm sure you've caught on, there are a number of ways to come up with your rules. I like to compare my old rule to my ideal one and then in between, instinctually think of the interstitial rules as I make and then test out each new one. But you can also identify your old rule, and then write new rules as different situations arise that prompt you to think of them; eventually, you'll land on your ideal rule or perhaps always leave it open-ended so that you can evolve with it. Another, really helpful option is to write down your old rule, your ideal rule, and then answer three very simple questions that help you determine any new rules in between. The questions are 1) Is this belief true? 2) Does this belief have to be true moving forward? 3) What can be a new truth that I can readily accept? The answer to your final question becomes your new rule.

Using the three questions is especially clarifying when you're updating a rule that's loaded with complicated history because it forces you to confront your current reality and formulate a rule that helps you navigate it in that moment. This makes me think of my client Geena who moved with her kids into her mother's small home during a financial struggle. After only two months, Geena and her mom were constantly rehashing their past grievances with each other and arguing about Geena's parenting techniques. Being in such close quarters under tremendous stress didn't help, and a year into this, Geena decided she needed to move her family out— but only felt comfortable doing this once she was on better terms with her mom. Geena realized that when it came to her mom, she'd been living by the old rule, "My mom is who she is and will never change," which was only giving Geena more grief. She decided that her ideal rule would be "I have a healed relationship with my mom," but also knew this wasn't immediately realistic. In between, Geena used the three questions to create her new rules. When her first old belief began to feel heavy and untrue, and she admitted that it didn't need to be true in the future, Geena changed her rule to "I can choose to act from a place of love when I'm tempted to yell at my mom." And when that began to feel untrue, she adjusted it to

"Nobody needs to be fixed at all, but we need to stop treating each other badly." From there, it was much easier for Geena to figure out the steps she needed to take to reach her ideal rule—a place of calm, mutual respect.

Using the three questions is also optimal when you are creating a new rule that contradicts long-standing values. I'll never forget a client named Faith whose son Brad was addicted to heroin. Faith always saw herself as a mom above all, and when she first came to me, she was constantly worried that she wasn't doing enough to help Brad. Though Faith had been trying to manifest a few things outside that relationship, like a new job and the money to build a new barn on her farm, Brad's addiction weighed so heavily on Faith that she needed to address this tangled energy before her other goals could transpire. Though it was painful, Faith decided to rewrite her rules around her relationship with Brad and his addiction, tucking a few action steps into her new rules to simplify her process. Faith's old rule was "A good mom does everything for her child," and she left her ideal rule open-ended. Realizing this was no longer true, Faith decided "A good mom does all she can without calling the police," moved to "A good mom does not give her child money but will buy him groceries," and when that last one felt untrue, "A good mom changes the locks on her house." Most recently, she decided "A good mom loves her son so much that she fully releases him so he can heal in whatever messy way it takes, because she's unconsciously playing a role in his illness." Living by this final rule has been the hardest thing Faith's ever had to do but it has surprisingly elevated the energy around her other goals and in conjunction with each rule revision, moved her closer to a stronger relationship with Brad.

When you make incremental rules from higher and higher mindsets, and put motion behind your rules, over time, you'll eventually rebuild your entire belief system until everything you want is possible to achieve. Rewriting your rules is a process that takes time, so as soon as you've begun living by your first or second rule and feel good about that, I suggest you flip to the next chapter about embodying your future self, the final secret we'll unlock together. Here, I'll teach you how to step into a future version of yourself that already lives the complete life you want, in all its worthwhile glory.

Tips and Takeaways

✦ Rewriting the rules is one of the final finishing touches on your ability to easily manifest.

✦ Decidedly naming and adjusting your rules is crucial because your mind needs mental constructs to work with, a map of parameters that guide you through your time on earth.

✦ When you change beliefs, your energy and brain reflect that. Good things often happen when you live on higher vibrations; whatever is available on those frequencies is easily accessible.

✦ Constantly reassessing your rules encourages you to move into higher vibrational realms.

✦ You can either rewrite rules deliberately or organically—or some intuitive combination of both.

✦ New rules fuel personal growth and fresh insight on how to add meaning and fulfilment to life.

✦ The more specific a rule, the easier it is for your mind to carry out and the universe to match it.

✦ When you make incremental rules from higher and higher mindsets and put motion behind your rules, you'll eventually rebuild your entire belief system until you have everything you want.

More Resources and Free Downloads

If you enjoyed this chapter, I've put together a downloadable pdf called "*How to Rewrite Your Rules and Beliefs*" that goes over my powerful process for rewiring your mind for success in just 5 minutes a day . Download it for free at www.authenticliving.com/gifts

Chapter 11

Secret #8

EMBODY YOUR FUTURE SELF

The last of my eight manifesting secrets is an incredible one-two punch. First, it's a shortcut to solving any arbitrary problems that get in the way of your goals, unexpectedly drop in your lap, and/or aim to interrupt your energetic groove from here on out. Second, it also teaches you how to step into positive, emboldening, and high-frequency personas when you set out to address these, or any other, concerns—and this further boosts your ability to co-create, in general. Teaching you how to embody your future self, then, is my final gift to you—a significant means of syncing up future desires with a high-vibing reality that colors your most radiant life. Like so many manifesting secrets, my last one requires a limitless mindset and deep conviction that all things are possible. At one time, this line of thinking might have felt corny or improbable. But after reading this book, I know you're open to the unthinkable since you're watching dreams manifest in real time. You know what's reasonable because you've made "the impossible" happen!

Consider how far you've come! In the name of manifesting a brilliant future, you've overhauled your psyche, healed low vibrational beliefs, and built fresh neuropathways in your brain to support more constructive beliefs, thoughts, and feelings. Your work has been fueled by learning how and when to check in with how you react to situations that either increase your happiness or subtract from it. You've learned how to break down the energy around harmful, core tenets and reframe them in a new light. You can now keep most of your emotional triggers at bay, practice self-love to add warmth to your day and lift your vibration, and send out the right intentional energy to support every meaningful goal and interaction you have. You know the most strategic means of setting a manifestation in motion, how to follow through with action steps that kick it into high gear, and how to tweak the ongoing rules that you live by so that you function on the highest possible vibration where the best choices and solutions are available.

In a word, you have achieved self-mastery. You know yourself more deeply than you ever have before, and with this comes the ability to not only recognize what sets you off but also how to create a gorgeous life for yourself—not despite your problems but in cooperation with them. When an issue shows up, you know exactly who you are and how to react in a healthy way that encourages growth and only adds to your capabilities. You have a peaceful command over your energy and psyche, who you are as a soul and a person. You're in alignment with the universe's best intentions and the highest good of all, allowing grace and abundance to flow.

In this chapter, I will help you access and learn from your future self and suggest how to tap into divine advice in real time by using this mindfulness- and meditation-driven technique. If you're stuck in a moment and don't know how to proceed, I teach my best manifesters that there is a version of you that's already done this and has the wisdom to know how to go about doing it well. To access this part of yourself, which I've dubbed your future self, you must go into a meditative state, call upon that version of yourself, and ask your future self how to solve your problem. We as humans are often so quick to become a victim of our circumstances or to throw our hands up in defeat, when in many ways, the answers and guidance we seek are already within us if we ask ourselves the right questions and trust the intuitive process that can unfold.

Changing Time and Space

When you embody your future self, you envision and become one with an enlightened version of you that has already figured out the concerns that you want to address. Your future self offers concise insight and action steps that show you the best way to arrive. Having access to this knowledge is reassuring since the process implies that there's a solution to every problem. Embracing this truth also means accepting unconventional notions of time and matter, but as an expert manifester, you know, firsthand, that the universe doesn't always operate the way you thought it did. It's entirely within your control to influence and shape everything around you.

I've channeled many times, and come to the wholehearted belief that when you direct your consciousness toward a certain goal, that creates your reality. After all, this is the overriding principle behind nearly all manifestation beliefs, including mine. Your thought frequencies impact particles in the universe, and if those particles vibrate at a high-enough rate, they become dense and are made into matter—that is, they become physical manifestations. As motivational coach Tony Robbins is known for saying, "Where focus goes, energy flows." I believe that our brains are so intricate that *we* are the factor that most dominantly shapes and impacts the world in which we live. In short: if you redirect your consciousness, you will redirect your reality.

Now when I refer to *future* manifestations, I do so because we live in a time construct.

But I don't believe that time exists in a linear way in which tomorrow is any different from today. This sounds a little like the plot of a sci-fi series, I know, but stay with me. In its simplest terms, I'm repeatedly shown that multiple realities are happening at once, but that we are not consciously aware of this because we view the world with a singular consciousness. The truth is the universe resembles an intricate hologram, built from our minds and projected outward. When we pour our consciousness into certain beliefs, thoughts, and feelings, they create the reality in which we exist— *until we choose to change it.* This is why working on your beliefs is so key to effectively materializing your aspirations when you're manifesting. Given all that, guess what happens when you embody a *future* version of yourself to solve a problem? That's right—you essentially jump into a new reality that's happening somewhere else in the universal hologram. But to get there, you have to follow the guidance of your future self, who already exists in this tandem world where the problem is already solved, in order to pull that vibration toward you. Once you complete the steps that your future self recommends, you and your future self are one.

Accessing Your Future Self Meditation

I like to use a simple meditation to meet and embody future versions of myself that are already living positive outcomes to my dilemmas in related universes. As you meditate, the more realistic this exercise feels, the more easily you will bring forth the frequency in which this problem is solved so that you can step into that future. Because your mind is connected to the universe, visualizations and meditations use the imagination as a bridge to creation, and reality can be built through these thought frequencies. Keep in mind that you want to make this mental and emotional experience so visceral, profound, and memorable that it's easy to reexperience and recognize in a conscious state. Meditating with as many senses as possible will always help.

To begin, take a few deep breaths to relax yourself and feel grounded to the earth beneath you. Imagine yourself walking into a white room where you see a large door in front of you. Open and walk through the door, and on the other side is your Sacred Space. Your Sacred Space is a corner of your imagination where you feel safe, calm, and loved. It can be on top of a mountain, near an ocean, on the sofa in your childhood home, under a tree . . . it's up to you. It can be a real place that you've visited before or one you've made up in your mind. My Sacred Space is fanciful and bright—it includes a live weeping willow tree that talks to me in a motherly tone, a crystal clear waterfall that spills into a beautiful lake, dolphins splashing about, lusciously green meadows, and technicolor flowers; most important of all, there's nobody else In my Sacred Place, other than me and my future self. In a word, it's my ultimate happy place.

Take a moment to settle into your Sacred Space and enjoy the way that this environment pleases all of your senses. When you're ready, in your mind, ask your future self to appear and approach you. Ultimately, they can stand in front of you or sit beside you—whatever is most comfortable. Now, briefly tell your future self what your problem is and ask them either what your next step or next few steps should be. The answer might come in a few digestible words, an instinctual feeling, and/ or a full-on conversation. Remember, this is a future version of you that already lives in a reality where the problem is solved, so you must trust their guidance. As you're in each other's company, notice as many details as you can about this other version of you. What does your future self look like? How old is your future self? What is their body type? What is their overall energy or mood like—optimistic, calm, confident? After about 10 minutes of conversation and observations, say good-bye to your future self and walk back through the door and into the white room again. Take a few deep breaths and open your eyes.

Asking the Right Questions, Receiving Guided Answers

Because your future self has the answer to any and every question you might have, no question is off-limits or process too intricate or general for their advice. I have clients who've used this exercise to discover and practice their spiritual gifts, land their dream job or climb the professional ladder, heal sibling schisms, solve parenting issues, and even cure writer's block or get over stage fright. You could also use this tool when you're at a crossroad with relationships or investment opportunities and brainstorming which routes lead to happiness and prosperity.

A truly inspired use of future-self meditations occurred with my client Joanne, who served in Afghanistan and suffered tremendous PTSD—this, from grueling combat experiences *and* being raped by one of her comrades. (Military sexual trauma, or MST, is shockingly common, particularly among female veterans.) When Joanne found herself triggered—and trust me, it didn't take much—she would use a future-self meditation to determine how a healed version of herself would respond to reminders from her past. Eventually, Joanne's future self gave way to a positive persona (I'll talk more about this in a bit) that she assumed in everyday life thathelped her deal with unexpected prompts like loud noises, upsetting stories told in her PTSD support group, and certain smells that reminded her of burning flesh or men's sweat. The good news is the last time I spoke to Joanne, she was impressively close to fully integrating with her future self and had begun using future-self meditations in hopes of starting an MST-related foundation. She's come so far!

When you do a future-self meditation and receive its guidance, be sure you're ready to make the most of the wisdom and insight that you receive. I've had more than a few clients who were hesitant to hear from their future self because they were afraid of, or not fully motivated to act on, the counsel that awaited them. Consider this: if your future self said that your first step toward emotional fulfillment was to leave your spouse or move to a new state, would you be ready to make those difficult changes? It's okay if you're not up for it; just know that the exercise won't work unless you are. Should the thought of truly tackling an issue shake you up, take it as a sign that you have some detangling and self-exploration to do first. Part of this work might include imagining what your current situation would look like, say 10 years down the road, if you didn't make the changes that your future self has suggested. This will help you better understand what's on the line for your happiness and consciousness. Then work on healing *why* you're not ready for answers rather than finding the answers. Once you've healed your hesitations, you'll feel much more inclined to follow your meditative guidance to a tee—and this creates rapid results.

Let's take a look at how a future-self meditation could play out in real life. So in meditation, you might ask yourself a general question that's been eating at you, say about your next steps toward happiness, or something more specific, like if you-in-10-years will still own your company. You can even ask about a large goal, like wanting to open a store or start an online service, with a series of meditations and the guidance that comes with them (when future-self exercises are used to help determine your manifestation action steps, as needed, they can potentially speed and amplify your results). For example, when I wanted to launch Authentic Living years ago, I often incorporated future-self meditations when creating my blueprint to determine what this version of myself would be like as well as what steps I needed to take to get my company off the ground. I was already a natural risk taker, but I did believe there was a version of me that already had a wildly successful business that helped millions of people around the globe—I just wasn't tapped into it yet. That belief acted like fuel to a rocket ship!

One time, I remember asking my future self what the most successful version of me looked like and was shown that she lived in a big, beautiful home where the window shades automatically opened as the sun rose, and there were luscious plants in every room of the house. She also had bright, healthy skin and appreciated the beauty in everyone around her. She was in her 40s when her achievements peaked. I also asked what my future self's actions were like outside of work and was shown that they incorporated daily journaling, kicking back with a beer, and having a very clear, direct way of communicating that almost came across as blunt.

I recognized enough of myself in these meditations to begin assuming this persona in real life so I could start pulling my future self's frequency toward me. Outside of meditation, I allowed myself to step into my future self by continuing to journal, taking better care of my skin, keeping my eye on real estate, speaking more concisely to employees, and exploring activities outside my comfort zone. Going about my day having adopted this new version of myself gave me a clear picture of who I was becoming and the business I was launching, complete with actionable, linear steps toward achieving both. With each new visit to the Sacred Space, I'd hear about new steps and take those strides—a bit like receiving and following the bread crumbs that the universe leaves for you when you're manifesting. Some steps were seemingly unrelated. I might have heard, "call your dad, and heal your relationship," or "go take a walk and then ask again." No matter what I felt, these instructions were all key to being able to build my future with a clean psychological state, soulful authenticity, and effortless manifestation goals. Eventually, I successfully launched my company—and in terms of my persona, I'm still becoming her. I do like to tap into this image when I need inspiration in daily life. For example, there was a time when I was working to establish better boundaries for myself. I tend to be overly empathetic toward others' problems, and I'd use a future-self persona to remind me that I don't need to get so involved in their emotions if it doesn't serve my highest self. So if I face a related conflict, I either present a question to my future self in meditation like *How can I respond in way that's unphased but still loving?* Or I assume the persona of a more boundary honoring version of me, and think *What would my future self do right now?*—and then act accordingly.

When you're in meditation, pay close attention to how it *feels* to be in the presence of your future self so that you can identify when you're acting this way and when you aren't. The more you behave like your future self, the more it will feed your dominant frequency until it's all you know. Louisa attended an event in Sedona because she wanted to figure out what her spiritual gifts were. When I sat with her, I immediately knew that a future-self meditation would help because it would be more empowering for her to find the answers than for me to give them to her. I taught Louisa how to meet the version of herself that was already practicing her spiritual gifts. In a meditative state, Louisa told me that her future self was carefree, unattached to financial gain, and deeply giving. Louisa also saw herself laying hands on strangers, so she knew her gift was to be a healer! She then asked this version of herself, *What are my next steps to practice my gift?* Without hesitation, Louisa saw herself traveling all over the world, practicing on anyone and everyone who needed her help. Not long after the workshop, Louisa and her boyfriend bought a van and the last I heard, they were on a cross-country road trip so she could perform lots of healings and not worry about paying her rent or a mortgage. During this time, Louisa said she'd mentally remind herself of what it felt like to be the woman in her future-self meditations—laid back, generous, and unattached to material goods—so that she could better pursue her purpose work and help the world.

I believe that tapping into your future self is about accessing divine, otherworldly knowledge. Perhaps when you call on your future self, you're transported to an energetic space where all answers and possibilities exist—and your future self acts as the messenger to help you become that version of yourself. I'm not sure, to be honest. Psychologist Carl Jung believed in a similar theory he termed "the collective unconscious" that he felt every one of us shares and is born with and that holds the answers to every problem we seek. He asserted that while we may not know what thoughts and images are in our collective unconscious, in moments of crisis, the psyche can tap into these solutions. He also thought the collective unconscious was the reason that the same fears and phobias could appear in children and adults with no explanation. He felt that specific symbols in dreams were dictated by the collective unconscious too, and could mean the same thing to different people. Nobody really knows! What *is* clear is that with any divine process, you must trust what comes through from your future self and be willing to act on it with faith for it to work. In a lot of ways, you're building strong, intuitive muscle as you do this, so perhaps there *is* a supremely divine force that's necessary to the process like I suspect.

The Mind's Role in Your Future Self

Tapping into your future self isn't just a spiritual or intellectual practice; it's very much a psychological exercise that toys with conscious self-development. What's more, I have seen it encourage neurological changes in the brain. Though I believe that when you meet your future self during meditation, you are truly encountering another version of yourself that exists in a tandem reality and dialing into that frequency, collaborating with your future self serves a second, very instrumental, biological purpose. The more you believe that a more enlightened, future version of you exists, and then act in a way that this edified future self does, the more you will habitually reinforce those improved behaviors and their neurological pathways. Your subsequent thoughts become the brain's automatic default, assuming that your behaviors are your current reality. It then requires less of a conscious effort to bring this persona into the future. This is different from a "fake it 'til you make it" or "acting as if" approach since your brain is already on board with your new behavior from spending time—both in a mental process like meditation and in real-life applications—cementing your new beliefs into actuality.

A lot of my clients like to name their improved future selves, just as you'd name an upsetting persona. I like to do this myself! In prior chapters, I talked about negative personas that come out to play when you're triggered. But as I'll bet you've noticed, when you take on the qualities and mindset of your future self, you're essentially creating a positive persona who knows how to behave when faced with a problem that they can expertly solve. It can help, then, to call on this persona by name if you ever need to solve a problem in a pinch and can't drop everything to meditate your way to a solution. We know that the universe is ever-expanding, which to me means that we are too; this leads me to believe that there are also versions of us that we have yet to "meet." So if your name is Judy and you're fighting with dad, you might tap into a future version of you that you've met while meditating about family issues, whom you named Zen Judy. Or if you're faced with a problem at work, you might slide into the shoes of Millionaire Judy, who's a wiz at solving professional issues. When you're in a tough spot, you can simply think *What would Zen Judy/Millionaire Judy do?*—and assume the mindset and behavior of that persona. Not only does this energetically connect you with your future self's frequency but also psychologically build a more capable version of you in real time.

Naming personas reminds me of Katherine, who was a thoughtful stepmom to an adorable seven-year-old named Doug. The child's biological mother was mentally unwell, so while Katherine was a secondary influence, she still took her job as a role model, responsible for shaping Doug's life, very seriously. One night while washing dishes, Doug told Katherine that his biological mom made a spiteful comment about how Katherine will "never be his real mom or love him as much as she does"—and how confused that made Doug feel because he said that he did, in fact, love Katherine as much as his biological mother. Katherine was furious, and though her instinct was to zap off an angry text to her husband's ex to tell her to let the kid feel how he wants, she remembered that she'd worked on her stepmom persona during a future-self meditation when she first got married. Here, she asked, *What's the version of me that—for the sake of my stepson—is conscious, receiving, communicating, and loving?*

Remembering how it felt to experience this persona, which Katherine appropriately named Capable Katherine, she was able to calm herself down. As Capable Katherine, she could see, now, that Doug's biological mom wasn't well and that Doug's health and happiness mattered more than any upsetting comments flung her way. Capable Katherine sat Doug down and explained to him that she loves him unconditionally and that he could call her whatever name he wanted. Capable Katherine then sent a thoughtful e-mail to Doug's mother, explaining what had happened. Though her husband's ex never responded, Katherine knew that she had handled the situation with grace and aplomb—and she had her future-self persona to thank for it.

At the end of the day, embodying your wisest and most enlightened self allows you to step into the inspiring success story that you've always been destined to become. Connecting with wisdom and counsel from your future self simply proves that once you've cleared all that is not part of your most authentic being, you've had the best and wisest answers in you all along.

Tips and Takeaways

✦ When you embody your future self, you envision and become one with an enlightened version of you that has already figured out the concerns that you want to address.

✦ When you direct your consciousness toward a certain goal, that creates your reality.

✦ In meditation, you can meet and embody future versions of yourself that are already living positive outcomes to your dilemmas in related universes.

✦ Your future self has the answer to any and every question you might have.

✦ When you do a future-self meditation and receive its guidance, be sure you're ready to execute the wisdom and insight you receive.

✦ When you're in a future-self meditation, pay attention to how it *feels* to be in the presence of your future self so that you can identify when you're acting this way and when you aren't.

✦ Tapping into your future self isn't just a spiritual or intellectual practice; it's a psychological exercise that toys with conscious self-development and neurological changes in the brain.

More Resources and Free Downloads

If you enjoyed this chapter, I've put together a powerful audio attunement called *"Activating and Embodying Your Higher Self"* that removes all blocks preventing you from accessing the wisdom, love, and manifestation abilities of your higher self today. Download it for free at www.authenticliving.com/gifts

Chapter 12

COMING
FULL CIRCLE

Once you've practiced and mastered the eight secrets, you'll notice that a remarkable and intuitive turn of events begins to unfold: You'll feel drawn to make this process your own. While you likely followed my instructions and examples to a tee when you were first learning how to create heartfelt manifestations, you now have an impressive foundation that will allow you to customize how you bring those goals to fruition. What an incredible evolution! Similar to when a person gets really good at playing an instrument or sport, you need to initially grasp the basics of manifestation before you can riff, improvise, and stylize moves that become uniquely yours.

Like so many of my most fulfilled clients, spiritual growth and manifestation will now urge you to lean hard on some secrets and omit others altogether. This is fine! In fact, I love when you choose to carve your own path because it means you've fully absorbed the practices in this book and are confident reinterpreting them based on a divine hunch and process that's led to success. Plus, everyone's programming and manifestation goals are different, so it makes sense that the practices that work best for you won't be entirely the same as what works for me. You can also expect that your manifestation MO will shift with each new goal you pursue due to the amount of detangling, self-love, intentional energy work, and so on, that you have to do first. If you're coasting along, with few cares in the world, then your process is going to look and feel a whole lot differently than if you've recently hit a speed bump. I find that if I just keep my eye on constant growth, with my arms wide open to receive whatever the universe has planned for me, then any manifestation process is at least underscored by this guiding and hopeful principle.

In this final chapter, I wanted to share a few of my clients' stories that speak to how far they've come and which tools and principles they lean on most while pursuing personal growth and manifestation goals. The eight secrets play a role in each and every story, though you'll see that these clients lean more heavily on some than others. You, too, are on your perfect path to internalizing these powerful secrets, recognizing which create the best outcomes for you, putting your own formula into play, and reveling in the benefits of deeply happy and fully realized experiences. I feel so blessed to say that my teachings have positively reset so many of my amazing clients' lives, and I 100 percent expect that they will change yours too!

Growing through Family Trauma

So many of my clients carry the burden of not just their own family wounds but a deeper, more ancestral trauma that's been passed down through generations—via inherited genes, long-held beliefs cloaked as "family values," and trapped energy that manages to seep into the client's programming and begs to be detangled. As you know, once you begin to heal these mental and energetic afflictions, your frequency rises alongside your confidence, self-love, and self-esteem. This yields consistent, positive experiences and interactions, which help sustain a higher vibration and pave the way for a much happier life and for spontaneous manifestations to occur.

When I first met Nicole at an event in 2019, she'd flown in from the Netherlands to see me after having taken a few of my online courses. From the moment she arrived at the retreat, Nicole said it felt like she was welcomed into a "new, warm family." At the time, a lack of self-confidence, low self-worth, and self-hatred were her greatest pain points. "When I tended not to do things well, I'd basically hit myself in the head with a pan. I felt like others couldn't see me for who I truly was at those times," she told me. Nicole's tendency to equate her actions and inactions with how others felt about her was a very deep-seated pattern with both ancestral roots from her mother and living in lack in her own life.

In terms of ancestral trauma, Nicole's mother survived a grueling experience in an Indonesian concentration camp during World War II—a painful experience that created a resolve to push through life's pain without discussing, understanding, or fully feeling or processing it. Nicole believes her grandmother was also an unhappy woman, trapped in a bad marriage. If that weren't enough, growing up, Nicole's sister was ill with diabetic ketoacidosis as a child, yet as an adult, became a successful business owner—and in both scenarios, received a lot of positive reinforcement and attention. Nicole's relationship with her mom and sister had always been strained as she felt she could never measure up to their expectations. She constantly craved maternal connection, and when she didn't feel it, defaulted to assuming she didn't deserve love. For years, Nicole found herself in constant fight-or-flight because of this. "I became hyper focused on doing things well to get the connection I wanted to feel, and when it didn't show up, I thought it meant I wasn't good enough," she said. "My family never said it outright, but I perceived it to be that way, and I internalized that conclusion." Nicole's feelings of inadequacy bled into every corner of her life—relationships, friends, work, social engagements. "It felt like everyone was taller than I was. But in time," she said, "I realized that I was actually *making myself* really small based on what I believed." Since Nicole's beliefs and programming stemmed both from a generational, energetic burden as well as a lack of self-worth that came from her upbringing, she set out to heal herself with the eight secrets plus dissolve the ancestral blocks that affected the many women in her family.

As an adult, Nicole went through a painful divorce with a man whose flaws she often overlooked and forgave. "I see the authentic soul in everyone, so I'd look through his self-centered behavior and find the good, which kept me loyal to him," she said. Nonetheless, he'd blame her when things went wrong and that perpetuated Nicole's poor self-image. "It was a huge struggle for me. I knew I was a good person who always tried to do the right thing. But being a good person didn't get me the love and connection that I needed from others, which I'd thought it would," she said. Financial and emotional repercussions set in after her divorce, causing Nicole to feel even more depleted and hopeless. Shortly after her decision to split from her ex, Nicole was diagnosed with stage 4 breast cancer and intuitively felt that her body had defaulted to a grave illness,because she wasn't honoring her most genuine self. The diagnosis further shined a light on Nicole's general discontentment and longing for more. She knew this was the universe's way of nudging her to make sweeping and life-changing decisions, once and for all. "I believe that all those years of feeling uncomfortable, tight, and craving answers to who I was manifested in cancer. Once I realized that, I began to see life differently," she said. "They were two heavy years, but every moment after was a realization that I had a new opportunity to choose me."

Through our work together, Nicole began to dissect the patterns and personas she'd been using to keep herself feeling safe. Up to this point, she'd lived in "survival mode" where her primary focus was on managing an unhealthy marriage; being a perfect daughter, sister, and mom; beating cancer; and simply getting herself to the next moment, the next day. The eight secrets, however, helped Nicole feel into her past, raise her vibration, and reinvent her life. She learned to reset her intentional energy and practice self-love. In fact, an alarm on her phone still goes off every four hours to remind her to take a deep breath, do a grounding exercise, go for a walk—and most importantly for Nicole, get out of her head and into her heart space. Because she has a tendency to help others while ignoring her own needs, Nicole also became more aware of this and how to correct it. Pattern interrupts like self-talk go a long way when she drops into old habits. "I tell myself, 'You are so good enough,' or 'I love you so much,'" she said. "I also use affirmations while I'm walking the dog. I match my words to my steps, saying, 'I am good,' 'I am calm,' and 'I am connected.' Synchronizing the energy of my words with what I want to create allows my being to tune in to it."

Nicole created a spiritual routine after the retreat that she still adheres to today. When she wakes up, she sets her intentions for the day, records her dreams and emotions in a journal, and "thanks all of the higher powers" for her family's health and the abundance that she believes is coming her way. While walking the dog or sitting on the beach, Nicole lets herself daydream about what she wants to create in the months ahead. "I tune in to the frequency of feeling what I want to bring into my reality," she said. When Nicole showers, she imagines the water cleansing her from all of her emotional and spiritual toxins, which then flow down the drain. During meditation, she imagines white and purple light, plus a golden liquid, coursing through her. Nicole finds peace in journaling, where she focuses on what she's feeling during the day rather than what's occurred since emotional awareness is a goal.

Nicole has a separate manifestation journal that she uses to record her aspirations. To date, they've all come to pass and have included becoming an international life coach, hosting live motivational events, traveling the world, and enhancing her relationship with her new husband. She's also manifested a better relationship between her ex-husband and son. "I live by a new set of rules now," she said. "I know I'm good enough. I'm worthy of being here and doing what I do. I've pulled myself out of guilt and shame, and I see now that love and connection are possible for me. I receive compliments and recognize that when things feel off, it's an opportunity for me to feel into that, expand it, and elevate it to a new level of consciousness."

Discovering and Standing in Your Truth

Once you deeply understand who you are, how your programming has led you to become the person you are, and how revising those beliefs can change your future? *Shoo*, kids. Your vibration soars, and major financial, emotional, and physical changes are yours for the taking!

What's interesting about my client Meleah's story is that her parents raised her on the ethos of a very famous self-help guru, with whom she later volunteered for eight years—yet despite having memorized all his teachings, she still felt unhappy and unfulfilled. After doing a 21-day guided audio meditation that she found online, Meleah serendipitously ran across my ads on Facebook. Meleah saw this as a sign from the universe that she should pursue my program and signed up the next day. "Messages about love really resonated with me as did the perspective that you can create the reality you desire," Meleah said. "I started to immediately see synchronicities and wasn't using half the self-help muscles I'd used before. I began releasing emotions and seeing change." Like a flash of inspiration, Meleah also realized that all self-development information she'd accumulated thus far meant nothing without the ability to integrate it with love. "I knew I needed to lovingly listen to my soul," she said. "This meant I had to stop people-pleasing and pursuing others' notion of the American Dream. The eight secrets shined a light on limiting beliefs that came from my past and needed to be reframed." For instance, when she misunderstood the way her father responded to one of her report cards when she was seven years old, it built the belief that Meleah wasn't good enough unless she earned the highest score possible and wouldn't earn others' approval and love unless she excelled. And then, years later, after an upsetting breakup, Meleah put on weight that she ultimately realized was the result of a subconscious belief that she could protect herself from future heartbreak if she didn't look her best and "padded" herself from the world.

Meleah worked through her programming as key insights surfaced, and she became a manifesting wiz. One of her most impressive feats happened after she recognized and detangled the false subconscious reel that her job would always be on the chopping block during company-wide layoffs because this had happened to her eight years prior. So when Meleah's new company announced that it would be going through changes, she didn't allow her fearful programming to stop her from creating a plan for them to keep her on board. Meleah stated her case, and she was instantly hired as a consultant; as a result, her bonus got a bump, she signed a retention fee covering more than two years, and her team grew— with a $30,000 pay increase, no less. "I stood in my authenticity and in doing so, I was rewarded in the high five figures. I spent seven years feeling like a failure, and in twenty minutes, rewrote what that meant in my life," she said. Meleah no longer sees herself as a failure or person who's unworthy of love but someone with the power to create her reality in every area of her life.

Shortly after her new post, Meleah got to the root of her weight issues and lost 70 pounds! She took control of her diet while working with a naturopath—then followed even more signs that led to a lifestyle overhaul. She cleaned out her house, began taking five-mile walks, and decided to start from scratch: "The weight melted off, with the majority gone in six months. The mental and physical changes that were happening redefined the whole tapestry of my life. It was a smooth and gentle ride. I'd stepped into the me that was there all along."

Turning Triggers into Opportunities

Getting in touch with what you're feeling, particularly when you're triggered, can transform a painful trauma into a remarkable opportunity for fresh growth and perspective. Personal choice—to decide how you wish to see your past, assimilate it into your consciousness, and use what you've learned from that to positively apply to your future—is an empowering tool that nearly all my clients incorporate into their manifestation practices, no matter their other steps.

Kelly was first drawn to my online program because it pleased her "science-y brain, with all that talk of pattern interrupts and rewiring. It made a lot of sense." Emotionally, she was desperate for direction as she was in the middle of a divorce while trying to climb out of welfare with a suicidal teenager, no less. Her past was peppered with all kinds of emotional, verbal, and sometimes physical abuse. "I was seeking," Kelly admitted, plus suffering from poor self-esteem, though she said she didn't realize it at the time. She just felt like bad things kept happening to her, over and over, and wanted to not only learn why but how to fix this glitch if she could.

By using the eight secrets, Kelly was able to set boundaries, let go of a precarious situation's outcome, and focus on her own growth. She decided that only those who wanted to be part of her path and grow alongside her, deserved to be part of her life. She appreciated that if she always made decisions for the highest good of all, the universe would take care of her.

Kelly initially set alarms for check-ins, which helped her identify what she felt at various parts of the day and then detangle the whys about how she got there. Right away, Kelly realized that her painful, subconscious reel was triggered more often than she ever realized. Just talking on the phone, for instance, caused Kelly a lot of anxiety, though she didn't know why. Through detangling exercises, Kelly realized that when she was three and a half years old, her father left her mom for a younger woman who had a son. And when she'd call her dad at his new home, she'd hear his girlfriend laughing in the background, with their little boy giggling along—and they all seemed so happy without her. She'd sing her father Stevie Wonder's "I Just Called to Say I Love You" because she didn't want him to feel upset living without her or guilty for leaving her and her mom behind. Kelly lived with her mom at the time, who was also an alcoholic, and soon, in and out of rehab; in time, though, Kelly moved in with her father and now-stepmom. "As I got older, I never knew if Mom was going to be drunk when she called," she confided. "I felt that I had to stay on the phone with her to make sure she was okay. I learned that this, combined with my initial calls to Dad, is why I had horrible energy around phone calls in general." Kelly even had trouble communicating with girlfriends and keeping up long-distance relationships because she'd clam up and disconnect on the phone. In time, Kelly was able to improve and forgive her relationship with her mom and view her childhood experiences more objectively and with an abundance of love. She's much more comfortable on the phone because she now understands and manages this trigger. "I believe that life hands us hard lessons that we're meant to move through," she said. "Phone calls presented me with lessons, over and over."

When triggers strike, pattern interrupts are a lifesaver for Kelly. "For a while, I moved my body, did jumping jacks, sang a little tune, took a hot bath—and then eventually, I could visualize snapping a finger in my mind to change my mood." Feeling misunderstood, say by a co-worker, family member, or friend, is another big trigger for Kelly, as it is for so many. When this happens, she asks herself why she's feeling the way she is and realizes she's assigning meaning to a situation that creates a belief *that's in her power to change*. "Learning to stop and realize that I can create new thoughts for a new reality was a huge epiphany for me," she said. "I don't want anxiety to be my reality."

At the heart of Kelly's perspective is a willingness to do things differently, which she says stems from self-love and a newfound worthiness. She releases the need for control and makes time for purposeful walks in nature, bubble baths, sitting in gratitude, and spending time in her infrared sauna. She avoids self-criticism and if she does spiral, she examines the situations that provoke this and reframes them. She no longer sees herself as a victim of circumstance and doesn't believe the actions and judgments of others. "I can choose how I feel about myself, for myself. I don't need to listen to other people's rules and thoughts and take them on as truth," she said. "They don't have to be my truth. I can make decisions about how I feel about myself."

Whether Kelly is manifesting or going about her day, she takes action based on intuitive guidance and which triggers continue to still show up. "The eight secrets have become part of me," she said. "It's a way of life now, and as I choose to implement the tools I've learned through these life-altering lessons, things just get better, more abundant, and more exciting."

Change Your Thoughts, Change the Future

Manifesting is an impossibility if one of the programming demons that you have to slay is deep and repeated forms of self-flagellation. Though the root of this issue often comes from outside influences, the fact that we reinforce this ourselves will always keep you in a sustained, low vibration until you make a conscious choice to change course. That's when your energy is in sync with the universe's and your combined frequencies really work their interrelated magic.

Mike's self-esteem was admittedly in the dumps when I met him, but he's one of my favorite success stories because his ongoing commitment to self-growth—and the manifestations that come from it—are so fun to witness. When Mike first found me, he struggled with confidence and negative self-talk. He worried over imposter syndrome, feeling unworthy, and had a hard time engaging with others. When he worked as a scientist, he'd attend seminars and then run back to his room to hide afterward. Mike was high up in his field, and though he'd often have a captive audience during his well-attended talks, he still feared that he secretly had no idea what he was doing and someone would figure out that it was all a load of bologna.

While learning the eight secrets, Mike realized that his brain was creating this false reality—and that if he chose, he could create a different one. "When I find myself slipping into negative mindsets and emotions, I can choose not to," he said. "I make the decision to change the channel, then I do. Sometimes I'll use 'I am' statements that are appropriate, sometimes I'll tell myself that I love myself. It also helps to remember that no matter how I feel about myself at that moment in time, someone else out there loves and accepts me the way that I am."

To Mike, manifesting is "simply getting out of your own way"—
though I know there's a much more energetic component to it than
that. And his new beliefs, which I feel have rewired his neurological
pathways, are part of his winning formula. Mike has manifested
both professional and personal achievements with ease and comfort. "When I stopped being a scientist, I considered consulting and
said, 'I want $140,000 in contracts before I do this,'" Mike said. "By
saying that, I had a vision of what I wanted and got to the point
where I had $120,000 in proposed contracts—but I'd have zero if I
hadn't determined where I wanted to go. I got out of my way, started
looking for what I wanted, and I found it. That's how it works." As
of this writing, he's also lost over 60 pounds after deciding to lose
weight! "I'd never felt like doing it before, but then I decided one
day that I would just like fruits and vegetables more than other
stuff, and eat mainly those, and I was going to be happy about it,"
he said. "I'm not struggling because I'm doing what I want." Mike
said he doesn't worry about what was keeping him in a bad spot;
it's a matter of choosing self-acceptance and a nonjudgmental perspective every day.

As for that initial shyness that kept him in his hotel room at
conferences? Mike now lives to network. "I love to meet people, talk
to them, and I have fun with it," he said. "If I'm not in the mood, I
replace that feeling by telling myself it will be fun." He adopts the
attitude he wants to feel. "I'll say, 'I'm going to have fun' since that's
what I want. Manifesting falls out of that."

Embracing Genuine Positivity

I always say that you can act as positive as you want, but if your
mind doesn't believe it, all those forced smiles and sunny perspectives won't mean a thing. You have to train the brain to truly believe and essentially override your negative programing with a more

positive and powerful experience. In turn, this tweaks your intentional energy and lifts your vibration.

My client Dianne is a manifesting pro—a pro, I tell you! She's mostly worked with my online programs where she was able to initially identify factors that held her back from reaching what she felt was her full potential. Professionally, she'd always jumped from one opportunity to another without knowing what she should be focusing on, and she never believed money could or should be easy for her to make. She also constantly worried about her emotional future since her past programming conditioned her to think that it was more likely that things would go wrong for her than right. So Dianne sought to revamp these limiting beliefs and achieve inner balance through my programs rather than wallow on where she felt she was falling short. She focused on becoming realistically positive, versus perfect, about her goals—and as a result, the universe blessed her with abundance galore.

After working with the eight secrets, Dianne realized that she'd created a persona based on how she grew up. Both of Dianne's parents are church ministers, and throughout her young life, she was taught to endlessly give to others, even if it overwhelmed or "emptied me," she said. "I grew up thinking that if people asked for help, and I turned them down, it was a sin." Dianne was also taught that whoever took her virginity was the man she should marry, so when she was raped by her first boyfriend, Dianne stayed with him for almost nine more years and endured his physical and verbal abuse; she felt that if she didn't marry him, she was worthless since she was no longer a virgin. "This relationship reinforced the belief that if others hurt me, I should let them. I turned the other cheek a lot," she said. Healing her complicated past meant seeing her parents, who were inevitably connected to her dysfunctional belief system, through a new, objective lens—and herself, in a different light. "At first, I had a hard time believing that my parents could unknowingly harm how I viewed myself because of how they raised me," she said. "My past created anchors that held me down in a lot of ways. But when I came to terms with this, I learned that I could become a bigger person without this persona. I went outside of who I was and saw what I needed to fix and let go of." Being positive about her future, personally and professionally, was a concerted choice, and practicing this built better neurological pathways.

Pattern interrupts were key to feeling genuinely upbeat about what tomorrow might bring. Any time Dianne fearfully anticipated the future, she'd stop her negative train of thought, sing a song that made her feel happy, and then tell herself to think of all the great stuff in her life that made her feel grateful. This progressed into regularly thinking about good things that were on their way to her and feeling that she *deserved* them. This last part was key to healing Dianne's beliefs since she'd previously struggled with viewing her needs as valuable. Having natural positivity made it easier for Dianne to believe in a bright future: "I eventually believed that everything would fall into place and that I deserved every good thing that happened and will happen to me."

In no time, Dianne genuinely accepted that she deserved self-love and superior treatment and that she didn't have to do something big to earn them. Her vibration soared, and so did her manifestations. "Now, I give what I can give because it makes me happy. I also ask for what I want, in real time and in manifestations, and because of that, I always get what I want. Sometimes, just by thinking intently." Dianne infuses everything she thinks and does with an extremely positive and inspiring love, which is so different from her conditioning: "It's a love that doesn't drain my cup. Love that will not end up hurting me. Love that makes my heart full."

So what has Dianne manifested? More like, what *hasn't* she manifested! New shoes, braces, a higher-paying job, a smooth surgical procedure, cars, her dream home by the sea, and her dream business (to name a few). To arrive here, she likes drawing pictures of her goals or taking photos of them with her camera. Then she prays for her desires and thanks God for bringing them to her because she ardently believes that God is already sending them her way. Finally, Diane visualizes herself in the context of her goals and takes action steps that "feel light and not heavy." She's also cut ties with people and opportunities that steal from her positive energy—and she never looks back. Subsequently, Dianne's life is her own incredible design.

"I always knew I was the solution to my own problems," she said, "but I never really looked in the mirror to realize who I wanted to be. So much has changed for the better and is continuing to do so. I credit the eight secrets as a huge part of who I am today."

Pursue Growth, No Matter What

One thing that I love so much about the eight secrets is that you don't need to be in a bad spot to make the most of them. You don't have to recognize that you're operating from a negative space, sense of lack, a poor self-image, or even faulty programming to benefit. It's enough to simply crave a better life and spiritual growth, and watch the pieces fall magically into place from there.

Carla initially signed up for my online program because she was on "a personal development journey." Then, as she delved deeper into the techniques, "things that needed addressing just automatically revealed themselves." In other words, the universe did its thing.

Carla told me that she's always been aware of her moods and feelings and their effect on her overall well-being, but that the eight secrets offered her a more intentional and structured approach to monitoring her vibration. Even so, she used the tools that worked for her and moved on from those that didn't. Though she never set check-in alarms, for instance, she did take her "emotional/vibrational temperature" throughout the day to help her access not just her feelings but her "feelings about her feelings"—that is, where they were coming from, why, and what to do with them, until she could narrow down an answer to help her put this new framework to use.

In no time, Carla realized that dense energies were surfacing to get her attention and provide an opportunity to work with and elevate them. "I learned that instead of lambasting myself for feeling negative, I should lovingly encourage the aspects of myself that experienced pain, confusion, or trauma, and give gentle assurances that we'd work through things together," she said. Carla decided she'd no longer be dismissive or frustrated with herself, which fostered an atmosphere of healing as well. And as she presented increased understanding and compassion to herself, she found that personas came to the fore—specifically, The People Pleaser, The Pushover, and The Victim—which set her on a path to understand, heal, and transform them. "I went to work to find out how these personas felt they were protecting me, and by unraveling this important information, I was able to replace them with healthy, higher-vibrational alternatives," she said. All the while, pattern interrupts like going for walks to clear her head and get her body moving plus spending time with pets were big go-tos. Meditation and vibration-oriented music and sounds like shamanic drumming and binaural beats have become regular practices too. All these tools help her catch negative emotions before they spiral into depression or helplessness.

Carla focuses on positive intentional energy and sustaining a high vibration both for her sanity and manifesting abilities. Though self-love has helped her heal from eating disorders and narcissistic relationships that overshadowed most of her life, she says all the secrets encouraged her to realize that she needed to be her "own best friend" to make life-preserving decisions going forward. She regularly raises her vibration by mentally listing all the things she's thankful for, spending time in nature and with her animals, listening to her favorite music, and savoring every experience right down to a cup of coffee or glass of wine on her patio. "I take care of how I feel as this is producing my now and tomorrow," she explained. "We have mind-blowing power as energetic beings and with that comes the responsibility and tremendous joy of deliberately directing our energy to manifest the incredible, fulfilling lives we came to this earth to embrace."

Carla's manifesting process specifically involves identifying her desires, consciously acknowledging that she's made from divine energy that exists within herself, visualizing the end scene of what she desires, and letting it all go. She also finds journaling to be a powerful means of focusing intention. Meditation helps her envelop herself in stillness and trust the process that's vital to letting go. She feels her way through action steps by determining whether they feel light or heavy. She says she's consistently manifested the people, circumstances, and resources she's needed to achieve every step of growth—financial, professional, and personal. She even dials into her future self when she faces a challenge. "I'll often imagine my future self explaining to friends how I received a promotion or how I set intentional energy for someone's healing only to have them call to tell me how much better they felt," she said. "One of my biggest ahas has been understanding that it's all done already. Anything we desire is already a reality and needs only for us to choose it for ourselves and establish itself in our reality."

Like so many of my beautiful clients that I deeply adore, everything that *you* imagine for yourself is just waiting to integrate itself with your reality. The eight secrets will help you manifest that future as will your own understanding, patience, focus, and intuition. It's my deepest wish that you now trust and believe that a healing and miraculous life is possible for you when you're ready to raise your energy and claim it. You deserve all that is good in this world and are worthy of receiving it in abundance. And in case no one has told you today . . . I love you.

Tips and Takeaways

✦ Use the foundation of the eight secrets to now make the manifesting process your own.

✦ Your vibration is ready to soar—with major financial, emotional, and physical changes ahead!

✦ Connecting with your feelings lets you transform painful trauma into growth and perspective.

✦ When you train the brain to believe and override your negative programming with a more positive and powerful experience, this tweaks your intentional energy and lifts your vibration.

✦ You don't need to be in a bad spot to benefit from the eight secrets. You can simply desire a better life and spiritual growth, and set the intention to feel and spread love by co-creating with God.

FINAL THOUGHTS

I write this while snuggled into a large, overstuffed love seat in my library, surrounded by too many books and unopened boxes from our recent move to Colorado. Despite the fact that the room is hardly decorated and desperately needs a rug, this is a sacred space for me. From where I sit, two floor-to-ceiling windows frame the majestic La Plata Mountains in the distance. Spring has arrived, and there's a crisp breeze that's gently blowing the plum trees and lavender bushes outside. Though I'm drawn to the landscape, this is not just a nice view for me. It is a manifestation come to life. The energy in and around our home is calm yet alive. No matter what the day brings or what mood I'm in, it feels good to be here. I'm right where I'm supposed to be.

For now, anyway.

We moved to our small town in Colorado because it is where God guided our family to be for the time being. Our life here stands in stark contrast to what it was when we lived in Laguna Beach, where celebrity friends joined us to watch the sun set over the Pacific and some of the best restaurants in the country were around the corner. I won't lie; I miss my Nobu. But Colorado is where we will raise our kids, continue to grow our business, meet new and heart-centered friends, help an increasing number of clients reach their fullest potential, and fulfill the meaningful calling of our souls. It is where I will continue to allow God's power to flow through me every day so that I can help others live their best lives.

No wonder I'm so at home here.

The funny thing is, feeling so content isn't the same as feeling like we've "arrived." It's actually the opposite for me. I feel energized to do more, as if I'm just getting started. When you have a manifesting mindset, you never stop creating. There's never an arrival. It's an ongoing evolution. My company has so many big plans, and we are growing by leaps and bounds.

I dreamed this wild and gorgeous dream, and I have consciously made it come true.

As you know by now, the manifesting secrets aren't just about getting what you want; they're about using inner growth to help you create the life you desire. When you choose to heal and nurture your inner world with love and integrity, your outer world will deeply and beautifully reflect that. Your life's scope becomes far greater than you ever imagined because your inner landscape is in flow with the world around you. Right now, my inner world is gorgeously mirrored in the towering mountains and lush greenery that surround me in Colorado. I have a loving relationship with my family and heartfelt connections with friends. I'm one with God. I live and breathe my truth, and that's reflected in my tangible, emotional, and spiritual worlds. Once you embrace *your* truth, you'll never want to close your eyes to what it yields either.

As I send you off into the world, I wholly wish for you to meet your most authentic self—one whose light is turned on so brilliantly that you never live in the dark again. Remember, too, that the eight secrets aren't about perfection, but progress. If you only get one percent better every day, you'll still achieve enormous growth and change in time because you're choosing self-mastery. Anyone who is lucky enough to buy this book and read it is absolutely able to have a beautiful life. If a concept doesn't resonate now, come back to it; it may make sense tomorrow.

Trust that you are divinely supported. Know that you are unconditionally loved by the universe and myself. And never settle for less than your own view of swaying plum trees and lavender bushes. I promise you with every breath I take: *you are worthy and you can manifest it all.*

A SPECIAL INVITATION
The 8 Secrets Community

Readers of this book have created an incredible tribe of souls all running toward their best life. With a deep desire to either change their lives, enhance their lives, or positively impact others, we work together to eliminate what holds us back from our most beautiful reality in the highest good of all.

As the creator and author of the *8 Secrets to Powerful Manifesting*, I know I owe my work to a divine source and to the souls that resonate with the work I am blessed to have flow through me. Through our Authentic Living Community, I have seen the power of the type of collective energy that thousands of souls growing together creates, and if I had an opportunity to bring more souls together on this planet in high vibrational manifesting, I certainly would answer the call. With the intention to serve, hold one another accountable, offer perspectives that the book teaches, love on one another, and lift each other up with the power of the knowledge in the book and beyond, I knew an online community would be an incredible haven of massive, beautiful, and everlasting change.

Does this sound appealing to you? Consider this your invitation to join us! Just go to authenticliving.com/family and request to join our group and share your intentions with like-minded souls that may have already read the book, are in the midst of reading, are revisiting certain teachings, or like you, are just getting started! I am known for creating some of the most supportive, nonjudgmental, and magical communities on social media, and my beautiful team and I will be in there posting, answering questions, and going live often to support you in what is not just a book but a new way of life. I can't wait to see your first post!

And in case no one has told you today . . . I love you.

A Gift for You

I am so grateful that you purchased this book and allowed me to be part of your meditation journey. As a thank you, I'd like to gift you this *10-minute Meditation for Manifesting Abundance Quickly* which can be found at: http://authenticliving.com/gifts

ACKNOWLEDGMENTS

I'd like to thank everyone who contributed to this book and my ability to share its message. Writing this has been a true gift, and I can only hope that you will find it a gift to read too.

To Kristina Grish, this labor of love would not have been made so beautifully possible without you. You allowed me to stay in my zone of genius, and I will cherish our conversations always.

To Laura Nolan, for guiding this process and welcoming me into the world of publishing with so much expertise.

To Reid Tracy, Patty Gift, and Melody Guy at Hay House: I have found a family in you all, and I am so grateful for the ease I feel in working with you.

To Anthony William, for supporting me in my purpose work and loving humanity so deeply.

To Marian Lizzi, a special woman who sparked the world's ability to receive this information and love.

To Oliver, my love, my rock, my everything that is good.

To Braydon, born from my heart, I am so happy that your soul found mine. And to Zion, whose angelic presence alone changes my world.

To Mom, for growing with me.

To Daddy, your pain was my purpose.

And to the thousands that I get to call my "soul family"—my Authentic Lifers, the embodiment and representation of my love for humanity and all that we *truly* are.

ABOUT THE AUTHOR

Mandy Morris is the founder of Authentic Living, an educational organization that has over 800,000 students in over 60 countries, with both online and in-person courses designed to help individuals rewire their mind, heart, and energy for total abundance in all aspects of life.

Mandy's science- and love-based methods for creating instant and lasting change have been studied, taught, and used all over the world by therapists and coaches. Currently, her certified coaches practice globally. Mandy worked in Scandinavia and the U.S. to study how an individual's brain patterns changed through her communicative therapy methodology, which focuses on getting to the root of a flawed belief to eliminate the symptomatic issues. Mandy works with childhood programming, sabotaging beliefs, trigger management, abusive relationships, trauma, the science of manifesting, and the law of attraction.

Giving back and changing lives is one of Mandy's biggest passions. In 2015 Mandy co-founded Hustle and Heart, a philanthropic initiative aimed at alleviating hunger and providing education, safety, health care, sanitary needs, food, housing, and farming equipment to hospitals, tribes, and the underprivileged in the Philippines. The work was so fulfilling she went on to co-found the Authentic Living Foundation, providing scholarships for various programs and events, as well as resources for battered women and children.

Mandy currently lives in Colorado with her husband, two sons, horses, dogs, and chickens near the Authentic Living Heartland, a sacred retreat center owned by Mandy and her husband for souls that come to learn, grow, and heal.

To learn more about Mandy, visit authenticliving.com

Photo of Mandy Morris: Hannah Rose Gray Photography

We hope you enjoyed this Hay House book. If you'd like to receive our online catalog featuring additional information on Hay House books and products, or if you'd like to find out more about the Hay Foundation, please contact:

Hay House, Inc., P.O. Box 5100, Carlsbad, CA 92018-5100
(760) 431-7695 or (800) 654-5126
(760) 431-6948 (fax) or (800) 650-5115 (fax)
www.hayhouse.com® • www.hayfoundation.org

———

Published in Australia by: Hay House Australia Pty. Ltd.,
18/36 Ralph St., Alexandria NSW 2015
Phone: 612-9669-4299 • *Fax:* 612-9669-4144
www.hayhouse.com.au

Published in the United Kingdom by: Hay House UK, Ltd.,
The Sixth Floor, Watson House, 54 Baker Street, London W1U 7BU
Phone: +44 (0)20 3927 7290 • *Fax:* +44 (0)20 3927 7291
www.hayhouse.co.uk

Published in India by: Hay House Publishers India,
Muskaan Complex, Plot No. 3, B-2, Vasant Kunj, New Delhi 110 070
Phone: 91-11-4176-1620 • *Fax:* 91-11-4176-1630
www.hayhouse.co.in

———

Access New Knowledge.
Anytime. Anywhere.

Learn and evolve at your own pace
with the world's leading experts.

www.hayhouseU.com